ADVANCE PRAISE FOR

Parallel Practices

"I do think Barbara Regenspan's work on teaching for social justice and using the arts (most particularly literature) is original and challenging. I even think she opens new pathways in our thinking about both teacher education and elementary classrooms. I am also moved and impressed by her insightful treatment of 'activism.' She avoids all the pitfalls of irrelevant ideology, 'political correctness,' etc., and always has in mind the age and developmental stages of the children affected, even as she holds in mind the requirements of parents and members of the community when it comes to the encouragement of understanding on a number of levels."

Maxine Greene, Professor of Philosophy and Education,
The Center for Educational Outreach and Innovation, Columbia University, New York

"At last, a book for teacher educators who seek understanding about the issues of social justice in education *and* look for guidance, examples, and activities to use in their own courses and programs. Barbara Regenspan is an experienced educator who clearly knows of what she writes. She is an intellectual with the heart of an activist. She clearly explains how to develop curriculum of inquiry and service. She provides numerous examples of children and teachers engaged in classroom practices of social justice while learning academic content and skills. This book will be a much-used companion to those who care deeply about promoting a wise and caring generation of students."

Carl D. Glickman, President, The Institute for Schools,
Education, and Democracy, Inc.,
Chair of The Program for School Improvement, and University Professor Emeritus
of Social Foundations of Education, The University of Georgia, Athens, Georgia

"*Parallel Practices* is an original piece of scholarship that makes intricate connections between heretofore disparate and unrelated realms of research and theory. Dr. Regenspan provides a pathway from the important—but too-often inaccessible and increasingly repetitive and dull—work of critical theory to a highly desirable teaching practice that is engaged, robust, and purposeful. Using autobiographical reflection, theoretical and qualitative inquiry, and field experiments, Dr. Regenspan makes a unique contribution to our knowledge about teaching teachers to value and engage issues of social justice in their practice."

William Ayers, Distinguished Professor of Education, Senior University Scholar,
Director, Center for Youth and Society, University of Illinois at Chicago

Parallel Practices

Studies in the
Postmodern Theory of Education

Joe L. Kincheloe and Shirley R. Steinberg
General Editors

Vol. 206

PETER LANG
New York • Washington, D.C./Baltimore • Bern
Frankfurt am Main • Berlin • Brussels • Vienna • Oxford

Barbara Regenspan

Parallel Practices

Social Justice-Focused Teacher Education and the Elementary School Classroom

PETER LANG
New York • Washington, D.C./Baltimore • Bern
Frankfurt am Main • Berlin • Brussels • Vienna • Oxford

Library of Congress Cataloging-in-Publication Data

Regenspan, Barbara.
Parallel practices: social justice-focused teacher education and
the elementary school classroom / Barbara Regenspan.
p. cm.—(Counterpoints; vol. 206)
Includes bibliographical references and index.
1.Social justice—Study and teaching (Elementary). 2. Education,
Elementary—Social aspects. 3. Elementary school teachers—Training of.
4. Postmodernism and education. 5. Dewey, John, 1859–1952.
I. Title. II. Counterpoints (New York, N.Y.); v. 206.
LC192.2 .R45   370.11'5—dc21   2002003924
ISBN 0-8204-5593-8
ISSN 1058-1634

Die Deutsche Bibliothek-CIP-Einheitsaufnahme

Regenspan, Barbara:
Parallel practices: social justice-focused teacher education and
the elementary school classroom / Barbara Regenspan.
–New York; Washington, D.C./Baltimore; Bern;
Frankfurt am Main; Berlin; Brussels; Vienna; Oxford: Lang.
(Counterpoints; Vol. 206)
ISBN 0-8204-5593-8

Cover design by Joni Holst

The paper in this book meets the guidelines for permanence and durability
of the Committee on Production Guidelines for Book Longevity
of the Council of Library Resources.

Printed in the United States of America

Contents

Acknowledgments   vii

Introduction: Parallel Practices: Social Justice–Focused
Teacher Education and the Elementary Classroom   1

Chapter One: The Author Re-evaluates Her Earliest Elementary Teaching Model in the Service of Prizing the Stuff of
John Dewey's "Human Life": How a Conception of
"Wholeness of Labor" Might Generate Parallel Practices
for Elementary Curriculum and Teacher Education Work   23

Chapter Two: Using Classic Social Reconstructionist Text in
Elementary Teacher Education: Study Guides and Lesson
Plans to Move Prospective Elementary Educators Beyond
Laissez-Faire Discussion Toward a Commitment to Social
Justice   45

Chapter Three: A Day in the Life of Social Reconstructionist
Arts-Based Teaching on a Multi-age Elementary Team:
Parallel Practices for the Elementary School Classroom   79

Chapter Four: Using Multicultural Literacy Assignments to
Inspire Social Action as Curriculum: Salman Rushdie's
Haroun and the Sea of Stories Illuminates My (A Teacher
Educator's) Community's Development Crisis   115

Chapter Five: EDUC 594: Social Action as Curriculum: From
Animal Dreams to the Museum of Social Advocacy as Art   135

Notes   171

References   173

Index   177

Acknowledgments

This book has evolved over many years through conversations, formal and informal, with family, friends, teachers, students, artists, and community activists. A very few of these people, those identified with first and last names, are acknowledged by way of being presented in its chapters enacting their own inspiring practices. Likewise, the work of named institutions is accurately described in the book.

Limits of space, time, and memory make it impossible to name the many others who have shaped my thinking and improved my practices. Still, a few individuals must be noted here: Monica Miller-Marsh, Judy Kugelmass, and, for a short but sparkling period of time, Emily Kudela, collaborated with me to build our Social Justice–Focused Master's Programs in Elementary Education in the School of Education and Human Development of SUNY Binghamton, where all of our colleagues, including Deans Linda Biemer and Ernie Rose, have been supportive of our work. Thanks as well to Wendy Kohli and Margaret Yonemura, who laid the foundations for our current philosophy and programs, and to Nancy Ziegenhagen and Carole Matruski, who have continually made their expertise and commitment available to us.

Although very different in scope and content, this book has its earliest roots in my unpublished dissertation, "The teacher as maternal storyteller: a revaluing of the ties that bind in the primary writing process classroom" (1994). That case study interpreted the conversations initiated during the whole group writing lessons by Sodus Central Primary Building classroom teacher Judith Davis, who is mentioned throughout this book. She is also one of a number of teachers who inspire the composite "character" Mrs. D. in Chapter 3, where Judith Davis's recently deceased Aunt Vy is featured in an authentic anecdote from my dissertation research. Priscilla Lawrence, partner of my first delightful co-teaching experience, also in Sodus, is inspiration for Mrs. D.'s interaction with Lashanda in Chapter 3's vignette #5.

Binghamton City School District teachers Laura Lamash (also a BU doctoral student), Lisa Rieger, and Renee Hoover, as well as Jim Hodges of the Susquehanna School, have provided models for me of the quality of collaboration of teachers in arts partnerships and community exploration featured in Chapter 3. Kay Embrey, director of the Cornell Migrant Program, is the friend who continually makes available resources around issues of migrant worker rights. Teachers Rebecca Godin, Arthur Baraf, and Ira Rabois, as faculty advisers at the Alternative Community School in Ithaca for the Eco-Action and Students for Social Responsibility committees, supported the commitment of their students to the solar panels advocacy project featured in Chapter 4. All student projects in Social Action as Curriculum featured in Chapter 5 have been supported by small grants from the Service Learning Institute of the Binghamton City Schools as well as one-time grants from Broome-Tioga BOCES and the Broome County Teacher Center. Two mural projects received support from Decentralization Grants of the New York State Council for the Arts.

Beverly Rainforth helped streamline the complex organization of Chapter 3 with humor and good cheer. Beth Burch, Ardie Gillespie, and Alison Levie vastly improved Chapter 4 with their editorial suggestions. Jack Goldman had inspired the earliest incarnation of that chapter through his gracious invitation to write for *Bookpress*. Graduate student Lizabeth Cain worked with me to shape the content of the museum brochure featured in Chapter 5 and kept me honest as well!

First Brian Ellerbeck, and then Carol Collins at Teachers College Press provided numerous encouraging reviews of earlier incarnations of this work and, along with Maxine Greene, Judy Greene, Irene Zahava, Maggie Goldsmith, Nancy Tittler, and Cathy Currier, gave me the confidence to maintain the idiosyncratic style of my presentation. Binghamton City School District teacher Sally Scarpino kept coming back to my Curriculum and Teaching in the Elementary Grades course, convincing me that my "parallel practices" were on the right track. Doctoral students Kate Bouman and Ellen Boesenburg were thoughtful and enthusiastic editors of my writing at different stages of this work. Graduate students Joyce Lewis and Laura Oliveto offered continual late-stage thoughtful and cheerful assistance.

Thanks to my former colleague at Binghamton, Joe DeVitas, who introduced me to Shirley Steinberg and Joe Kincheloe at Lang. Thanks to Morgan Brilliant of Trumansburg for her patient formatting and Jane Dieckmann, the most sought-after indexer in the Southern Tier, for her gracious style of work. Julie Quinn and Diane Hinckley, education department secretaries in the School of Education and Human Development at SUNY Binghamton, have supplied daily kindness, raucous humor, and competence.

Special thanks to colleagues Robert Carpenter and Beverly Rainforth for the writing support group in which this book got off the ground, and to UUP and Binghamton University for the Nuala Drescher Affirmative Action Leave that kept it soaring.

Finally, David Regenspan, my beloved writer-in-lifetime-residence, and Ben and Sarah Regenspan, my children, continue to nurture my vision of the "healthy conception of human development that the phenomenon of oppression distorts," which is at the core of this book.

Also thanks to:

Brookes Publishing Co. for permission to reprint from:
Regenspan, B. "Inclusive education through the arts in a collaborative community-responsive elementary team: A day in the life." In Beverly Rainforth and Judy Kugelmass, eds., *Systematic Approaches to Constructivist Practices*. Brookes Publishing Co. (for probable Spring 2003 publication).

Elsevier for permission to reprint from:
Regenspan, B. Toward parallel practices for social justice-focused teacher education and the elementary school classroom:

Learning lessons from Dewey's critique of the division of labor. *Teaching and Teacher Education*. Summer 2002.

Blackwell for permission to reprint from:
Regenspan, B. Moving elementary educators beyond laissez-faire discussion toward a commitment to social justice: Lesson plans for *The dialectic of freedom*. *Curriculum Inquiry*. Spring 1999.

Caddogap Press for permission to reprint from:
Regenspan, B. A teacher educator traces the roots of EDUC 594: Social Action as Curriculum from her initial student teaching experience: The road from Mrs. D.'s classroom to "The Museum of Social Advocacy as Art." *Taboo: The Journal of Culture and Education*. Summer 2001.

The Southeast Regional Association of Teacher Educators for permission to reprint from:
Regenspan, B. Using multicultural literacy assignments to inspire Social Action as Curriculum: A teacher educator uses Salman Rushdie's "Haroun and the sea of stories" to illuminate her community's development crisis. SRATE Journal (*The Journal of the Southeastern Regional Association of Teacher Educators*). Summer 2001.

Introduction
Parallel Practices:
Social Justice–Focused Teacher Education and the Elementary Classroom

I have long believed the truism that no matter what the subject matter you intend to teach others, you can really only teach who you are. What I learned writing *Parallel Practices* is that it is also the case that you can only *write* who you are. This book is a record of my developing thinking over a number of years as a social justice–focused teacher and teacher educator. It is a first-person, often autobiographical account of my efforts to do the work of elementary teacher education by way of consistently pursuing the inquiry, What kind of human life do we want social equity to make possible?

This question first came alive to me as a legitimate basis for the parallel practices of elementary education and elementary teacher education in my student teaching placement in a rural public school with second-grade teacher Judith Davis in 1972. At the University of Rochester, where undergraduates were prohibited from majoring in education, I had majored in Foreign Literature with a concentration in Russian, both because of my interest in the Russian Revolution and because of my love of nineteenth-century Russian literature. But I was able to earn elementary teacher certification through an undergraduate minor that allowed me to student teach with Judith Davis during much of my senior year. Judith Davis's "Primary Building" was in an upstate New York town where apples were picked by migrant workers whose children attended our school from September to Halloween. The school drew children from a ninety-square mile high-poverty region.

The educational philosopher Chuck Bowers (1987) would have

called Judith Davis "philosophically conservative." Although I saw myself as politically progressive, she was clearly one of the most powerfully educative forces in my life, reinforcing my intimation that elementary education could be a compelling, continually interrupted conversation for making sense of life, punctuated by regular explosions of life itself. It had a lot in common with nineteenth-century Russian literature.

I was hired to teach in Judith Davis's school immediately following my student teaching, as a multi-age primary teacher. Intellectually stimulating conversation around purposeful activity, her model, was the rich conception of the work that I brought with me into my own classroom. Very early on I showed my six through eight year olds how in the Cyrillic alphabet the Russian word for "dream" was the word for "nose" spelled backward. After I explained that this word play inspired Gogol's famous story, "The Nose," the children asked to hear that story, and I remember the joy of reading it to them in segments after recess. They listened in awe to the unexpurgated words of Gogol, completely fascinated by the symbolism of the main character being a nose with a pimple on it/him. The children were quite clear that this character was less than a whole person in the author's eyes. We had fascinating conversations about why this was the case, and we ended up talking about bureaucracies as environments that encouraged people to be afraid to take risks. We explored very big ideas in young children's language: disembodiment and fear and personification and greed.

I also remember that we wrote stories that had a body part as a main character. So I was introduced to Mr. Butt by six-year-old J., long before Salman Rushdie formally wrote into the world this powerful citizen-philosopher with *Haroun and the Sea of Stories*, featured in Chapter 4 of this book.

Although I believe that the cooperating teacher with whom I worked in upstate New York in 1972 was an unusual person and educator, I also believe that the rich definition of my role as a student teacher, then teacher, was less rare in that historical era than in this current one. In both my teacher education program at the University of Rochester and in my placement, "taking dictation" from children and "invented spelling" already existed, but they did not have formal names and were not presented to me as methods of "literacy instruction." They were commonsense tools for giving children a voice to write down what they wanted and needed to communicate to the rest of us. And because exciting artifacts of the world were continually introduced into the classroom, there was always strong desire to communicate on the part of the children. We experienced our share of challenging behavior, but never saw a need for "character education." Judith Davis reinforced what I had learned at the University of Rochester: character education happened when you critically studied literature and history in the community of the classroom and when you played at the water table without soaking the rug and gave your friend the words she needed to write down her observation on the science lab sheet.

It was also the case that "policy" involving communication with the parent community was flexible and very much reciprocally negotiated. When a combination of working-class and middle-class parents objected to stories coming home with incorrect spelling, a number of teachers shared the following rationale for a new (to me) practice: Many of the children we taught were not immersed in the written word when they left us, and it was clear that not all of their (what we now call) spelling "approximations" were going to improve quickly enough for them to get the positive support for their schoolwork that they (and we) needed from the families at home. So we gave the children twenty-six 3-by-5 cards held together by a binder ring or pipecleaner so they could wear a wordbook on belts they made in the art area (featured in every classroom) and they could "ask for" the words they couldn't spell conventionally. Related, many of us required of the children the memorization of a reasonable number of spelling words while establishing clear policy about what work could go home versus the "in-process" work that should stay in school.

We also used the generating of lists of rhyming words to help kids write funnier poems as well as to improve their spelling and reading; these were transitional activities between mask-making and cooking and junk sculpture inventions in the art area and the recording and transcribing of puppet shows and science experiments out in the hallway. But I had also learned from Judith Davis how to teach what Lisa Delpit (1995) now calls, "the codes of the culture of power" in clearly mapped-out blocks of time named "practice for reading and math." I had internalized Judith Davis's voice of intellectually inspired pragmatism, and it continues to speak to me: "J. clearly needs more work with phonics. Go get a few linguistic readers from the closet and let's group him with L. and R. for a while." "S. reads almost purely by whole word recognition. Let's get her started with a filebox and we'll use organic reading (Ashton-Warner, 1963) with her. That should work with T. and P. as well." "Keep R. busy with important errands, making new signs for the frog tank, and drawing when his group is using their Ginn workbooks. Workbooks don't mean anything to him, and he finds them boring. Let's not make a resistant reader out of him; he's a wonderful artist."

It's important to note that there was continual reinforcement for Judith Davis's intelligent voice by other adults in that school. When I narrated in the teachers' room the story about reading Gogol to my kids, a fellow teacher, Jim Wood, spoke to me about his literacy curriculum that used the children's dreams as text, a curriculum that would later translate into his doctoral dissertation, also at the University of Rochester. Urban-Rural grant money was available at that time and it was used to hire a former British Infant School principal to consult with us. Mr. Vines spent two mornings per week in my classroom. He taught me to teach a group of resistant writers how to use calligraphy pens, and he had them making gorgeous signs announcing the setting changes for their tape-recorded puppet shows. He even found a group of middle schoolers willing to transcribe from the tape recorders for us so the children could read their own scripts.

Mr. Vines objected in principle to my sending J. to the office for throwing a jar of paint at the wall, insisting that I had to learn to teach every child who came to me. He determined to teach me how to "tame the monster in J." through a combination of enforcing natural consequences of children's behavior in the classroom and by putting J. in charge of keeping supplies organized for science experiments and art projects, including writing purchase orders when we ran out of things. He taught me how to get a large group to dictate a coherent collective story by thinking up my own narrative format. He encouraged me to have French, Spanish, German, and Russian dictionaries in the book display case and to search for translations into many different languages of children's literature classics like *Goodnight Moon* (1947) and *The Runaway Bunny* (1942).

Today, I teach my students this practice of having children's books available in many languages as one of hundreds of continually negotiable *methods*. (I even teach them the format for collective story-writing that I came up with in response to Mr. Vines's directive to invent one: *Identify a specific community of people, animals, or aliens. What is the problem that their community is experiencing? Now use the rest of the story to show how the community comes together to solve the problem.*) But I specifically articulate to my current students that these methods are not to be confused with the most important issues, such as whether their classrooms resonate with Dewey's conception of "human life" (see Chapter 1) and whether the children are getting enough physical activity to pay appropriate attention.

Perhaps a certainty that the themes of nineteenth-century Russian literature are perfectly appropriate for the elementary school classroom is a very unusual way of thinking. Even I believe that a perfectly wonderful elementary classroom might be lacking dictionaries in seven languages. Perhaps not every teacher needs to know how to help the whole group dictate a collective coherent story. Our goal of three thematically linked science experiments per week might have been too ambitious. Still, the increasing absence of almost any big, imaginative ideas from the majority of public elementary school classrooms in the current historical era is very troubling.

For John Dewey, the division of labor between cultured people and workers was antithetical to the nature of human beings, 99 percent of whom were not distinctly intellectual but rather wanted to use their imaginations to design a work and social life that made sense in the context of living in a democratic community. I am interested in the implications for teacher education of two realities I typically observe in my students relative to our (very focused) study of Dewey: The first is that they readily, even delightedly, identify with, both for the sake of themselves and their own students, the above conception of Dewey's about how people want to use our imaginations. The second is that having grown up in a dramatically more multinational-dominated corporate culture than I did, they have had less access than myself and my peers to models of work, community cooperation, or political organizing that defy the division of labor. Although it may not be entirely conscious, the choice to teach appeals to many of them because they sense the enlivening potential in doing work that integrates making and thinking in the complex context of continually crossing cultural borders. They want the opportunity to enact (particularly with the socially marginalized young people whose needs our program emphasizes) Dewey's very rich conception of human imagination. But they have not grown up with an emerging labor movement, socialist movement, or public campaigns to pass national legislation opposing war as Dewey did; they did not grow up in the Civil Rights movement, the antiwar movement, or the militant feminist movements as I did; their imaginations, in the Deweyan sense, are typically more limited. I believe that this latter reality explains their tendency to initially identify with the more technocratic role for teachers modeled in schools, notwithstanding their earnest intentions to play out that role with creativity and compassion.

> We now have the abnormal situation that, in the face of the extraordinary novelties and complexities of modern times, there is no persuasive program for social reconstruction, thought up by many minds, corrected by endless criticism, made practical by much political activity. . . . The young are honorable and see the problems, but they don't know anything because we have not taught them anything. (Paul Goodman, *New York Times Magazine*, February 25, 1968)

In 1968, when this quotation originally appeared, I was a high school senior in Philadelphia, one of the honorable young who didn't know anything. In retrospect, I can see that by virtue of being a lower-middle-class Jewish teenager of that era growing up with class-conscious parents in a northeastern city, I *knew* (borrowing Goodman's meaning) a lot more than many of my current students do, which offers an ironic perspective on the notion of "privilege" and "privileged education." Excited by the black power and anti-war movements of the time, I went with friends to meetings for Philadelphia Students for a Free Society and even to study groups hosted after school right in my public high school, the Philadelphia High School for Girls. Years later I figured out what I'm sure our principal at the time did not know. These study groups led by Youth Interested (YI), were part of the Communist Party's front-group-building strategy. It was a very different historical era than the one in which most of my current students attended high school!

With such models of political education in my past, after teaching in Judith Davis's school for three years, I hungered for an urban environment and a more ethnically diverse cultural context in which to make sense of my experiences. So I left for New York City, initially to participate in the Summer Immersion Experience of Lillian Weber's Workshop Center for Open Education at City College. At the Workshop Center, my group negotiated for ourselves the project of painting on the corrugated metal wall of a City College annex at 137th Street and Convent Avenue, along with children who lived in the neighborhood, a mural called "The Cultural History of Harlem." My individual assignment was to study, sketch, and represent wherever appropriate on the mural the elaborate iron grillwork that was a standard feature of Harlem architecture, and also to symbolize in one corner of the mural the Studio Museum of Harlem, an artists' studio space and teaching cooperative.

I fell in love with New York and was delighted to be able to get a job teaching four year olds in a public daycare center in the Bronx, making it possible to stay beyond that summer and to continue to teach socially marginalized children. It was during the infamous "New York City fiscal crisis" and I became more radicalized politically, briefly joining a tiny Trotskyist organization called the International Workers Party. While a member of the IWP, I shaped the assignment that made sense to me and that I was best positioned to carry out: organizing in the Bronx, where

I was teaching my four year olds, a chapter of the then powerful Manhattan- and Brooklyn-based coalition Workers and Parents United for Daycare. Through that self-selected assignment I was able to inspire activism among the parents who knew me through my work with their children, activism that successfully brought public attention to acts of political corruption that were draining New York City's daycare resources. By continually calling attention to the "direct lease scandal," a collusion between real estate developers and their cronies in city government, Workers and Parents United for Daycare was a significant force in the successful parent- and teacher-driven movement to keep open in poor and working class neighborhoods daycare centers slated for closure by the bankrupt city.

It was during a huge demonstration and sit-in at the Mayor's office, well attended by members of our new Bronx chapter of Workers and Parents United for Daycare that I learned one of the important lessons that inspired this book. At that demonstration I stood alongside families who trusted my belief in this organizing effort in large part because they trusted my work with their children. Maria, who stood right next to me in the crowd of hundreds, was the mother of four-year-old Violetta and daughter of Pop-pop. Violetta's story, "How Pop-pop came here from Puerto Rico and was frightened by lightning on the boat," was dictated to me just the day before and now graced the big story wall that faced you when you entered our classroom. We had hatched chickens together last month. Maria had even come in during weekends with Violetta to turn the eggs. I had eaten at their dinner table where I had playfully supported Maria in battling her husband Tomas's machismo with my own accounts of my father's Jewish and Eastern European variety of chauvinism. I had also listened to Tomas's story of disappointment after disappointment in the work opportunities available to him. While genuinely moved by Tomas's experience, I was also collecting the intimate data about the wrong-headedness of the division of labor that would help shape my current approach to using the work of John Dewey with my teacher education students. (See Chapters 1, 2, and 4.)

It was the *visceral* quality of the connections with families, including Maria's, that alerted me to their disruption at that demonstration when, without my foreknowledge, fellow International Workers Party members positioned right beside me a huge red silk banner with black letters saying "Free Daycare for Everyone as in the Soviet Union, Cuba, and China." To make room for that banner, I, "my families," and fellow teachers from my daycare center were packed even more tightly together in that crowded space.

Interestingly, many of the same parents of the children I taught who stood beside me at the demonstration had been part of a study group convened just days earlier through our new Bronx chapter of Workers and Parents United for Daycare. At that meeting we had read and discussed some excellent literature about the history of daycare in the United States. The facilitator of the discussion and supplier of the literature was a local daycare teacher who was open about his membership in the Puerto Rican Socialist Party; his interpretations clearly resonated with all present. It was no surprise to any of the parents of the children I taught that daycare had been historically made available and withdrawn to suit the needs of what the literature and we confidently labeled "the capitalist class"; further, these same families were quick to identify this same class with responsibility for the billboards on the beaches of Puerto Rico that had lured their parents and grandparents with the slogan "Come to the U.S. and Earn a Buck an Hour." Likewise, the same social class interests were now threatening the availability of subsidized daycare that enabled many of the mothers in our group to continue going to college.

But these realities did not change the fact that the parents of the children I was teaching were not willing to associate me personally with "communism" as in the Soviet Union, Cuba, and China. My membership in the IWP suddenly raised questions about my motivation and sincerity in my interactions with their children and in the hours of delightful conversation I had shared with them. I left the International Workers Party shortly after this incident, characterizing too much of the organization's behavior as manipulative and sexist, and too much of its "theory" as romanticized. And even though I continued to work with great commitment both as a teacher of their children and as an organizer for Workers and Parents United for Daycare, some of the families of my four year olds never had the same level of trust for me again.

In the past few years I have begun to associate some of the critical theorists and feminist post-structuralists in progressive teacher education and related fields, including cultural studies and progressive foundations of education, with the IWP members who brought that banner to the demonstration. The analogy is captured in the citations from Dewey that introduce Chapter 1: Briefly summarized, his words assert that the production of ever-more-fine-tuned theory that nobody moves to enact serves only to "purvey cynicism." I have feared "catching" that cynicism myself from self-identified critical theorist colleagues who often wear it as depression, a state of mind that sometimes translates into "collegial" relationships lacking in generosity of spirit. Yet this negative identification on my part co-exists with a sincere gratefulness for the useful education offered me in the writings of these same critical theorists and feminist post-structuralists. During my doctoral studies at the University of Rochester, their work refocused my radical political education on public schooling; as well, their insights, selectively employed, continue to positively influence my teaching.

In order to explain my perception of the problem I identify in some of the current text-based "progressive" foundational work in education, I need to explain what I believe my own "education" gave me that critical theory and feminist post-structuralist text can actually undermine. When in 1977 I wrote down Violetta's story, "How Pop-pop came here from Puerto Rico and was frightened by lightning on the boat," I was educated by her on a level that far surpassed an intellectual comprehension of issues of social oppression. In fact, I now characterize the level of my education as *visceral*.

The effect of this visceral education was that before I went to bed at night when I reread the literature about the history of daycare interpreted by the Puerto Rican Socialist Party, I was thinking simultaneously about Violetta's Pop-pop's scary journey from Puerto Rico and the life of the migrant workers' children in the camps in upstate New York and even my own father's emigration from pre-Nazi Romania, which in his telling highlighted the smell of a steak, the first he'd ever eaten, in Thessalonica. I didn't separate what I at that time conceived of as the necessary defeat of the capitalist class from my *visceral* education. In fact, when I read the sophisticated historical and political analysis of the Puerto Rican Socialist Party, I processed the content *through* it. The words filtered through Violetta's love for Pop-pop that allowed her four-year-old self to conceive of his fear on that journey. They filtered through the memory of a particular child from a migrant family repeatedly touching the word "apple" on the chart paper that held the story she had dictated to me. (See Chapter 1.) And they filtered through my love for my own father that allowed me to smell the steak in Thessalonica.

When I am being successful in my current work in teacher education, *visceral* connections with text come alive in class. In trying to convey to my students an understanding of the homogenizing influence of "dominant culture" norms on curriculum, I feel a need to inspire that same look of complete engagement on some of their faces as the one on Violetta's face when she was narrating the story about Pop-pop and the lightning, or to replicate the laughter of Maria and myself in her kitchen after dinner, or the seriousness of my own attention to Tomas when he narrated his repeated disappointments with the labor market. I am convinced that the impulse toward activist response is ignited by a quality of engagement that is *visceral*. Again, I see that child smudging the word "apple" on the way to reading it.

In 1990 I returned to Judith Davis's classroom to do my research for my doctoral dissertation, convinced that participant observation in her classroom could help me develop this intimation of mine about the connection between *visceral* engagement and the impulse to act against what Maxine Greene called "obstacles" (1988). I wanted to explore the connection for its implications relative to social reconstructionist teaching in both teacher education and the elementary classroom. As I initially studied Judith Davis's orchestration of classroom talk during the whole group lessons that preceded individual and small group writing time, I observed that her often extended introductions to writing workshop typically engaged the children I described as "socially stressed" in particular. Further, the participation of these children in the conversation frequently inspired more energetic than usual forays into individual and/or collective writing.

A convergence of theory from diverse fields including post-structuralist literary criticism and autobiographical/narrative inquiry during the early 1990s made sense of these observations, confirming what Judith Davis clearly understood: that self does not generate autobiographical memories. Rather the reverse is the case. In the words of Craig Barclay and his co-researcher, Rosemary Hodges (1990), "The self is composed anew" in each presentation of autobiographical information.

I reasoned that this appreciation of the power inherent in "each presentation of autobiographical information" had dramatic implications for the teacher/researcher focusing on issues of social hurt as it affected the identities and learning habits of the members of the community of writers now identified with the elementary school reading-writing classroom. If teachers could help to shape autobiographies that contradicted messages of oppression and internalized oppression, the implications were that they were shaping people who could do the same.

I was finally able to complete my dissertation in 1994 because Sara Ruddick's (1989) conception of "maternal thinking/storytelling" offered a kind of political bridge to my visceral concerns:

> As she pieces her children's days together, a mother creates for herself and her children the confidence that the children have a life, very much their own and inextricably connected with others. (p. 98)

For Ruddick, a mother's stories reflect the balance between that aspect of the child's life that represents a separate quest, indeed, a separating quest, and the often marginalized other growth project of learning to appreciate and face the reality of one's inextricable connections to others. Given the compelling feminist perspective of Madeleine Grumet (1988) and other educators and researchers that the prototype for teaching is mothering, Ruddick's formulation appeared to capture the empowering balance of attention required in maternal work that also characterized many of Judith Davis's literacy lessons with her seven- and eight-year-old students.

The respect for *viscerality* in Ruddick's work was typified by her clarification of her conception of the child's "developing spirit." More recently I have come to appreciate how it adds a feminist complement to Dewey's conception of "mind-body" (see Chapter 1):

> The term "spirit" may be misleading. To speak paradoxically, from a maternal perspective the spirit is material. A child's body, from its birth, is enspirited. A primary experience of preservative love is an admiring wonder at what a new body does. An enspirited body is, in turn, a source and focus of mental life. From children's perspective, "bodies," both their own and others', provide some of the most poignant fantasies and puzzles of mental life. As children name, desire, avoid, or touch bodies, the bodies become resonant with "spiritual" significance. (p. 83)

The connection-making Ruddick accomplished between the body and our society's privileging of separation over connectedness invited in, although she herself avoided it in her own theorizing, a psychoanalytic feminist critique of oedipal resolution in a patriarchal society. This invitation allowed me to consider the thinking of psychoanalytic feminists Jessica Benjamin (1988) and Susan Suleiman (1990), both of them so lyrical that their work resonated with the spiritual content that I had no words for of Judith Davis's literacy lessons. Susan Suleiman specifically theorized the special positioning of mothers in relation to language, irreverently developing the characterization of "the laughing mother," which I was able to transform into "the laughing teacher." So the introduction of psychological theories into my grounding research allowed an honest break with a primarily political characterization of Judith Davis's work with the children and addressed my own discomfort about not quite capturing what was most compelling to me about that work.

For the purposes of the dissertation I interpreted that Judith Davis was a laughing maternal storyteller for the other people's children in her classroom. A writer herself, an avid reader, local history enthusiast, and teachers' union activist, though a philosophical and sometimes political conservative, Judith Davis managed to both draw out the "life, very much their own" of her young students and to help them see their "inextricable connected[ness]" by joyfully connecting the children's verbal and creative contributions through an association with *some* community—either their geographic community on a lake in upstate New York, or their personal community of family and friends, or the community of knowers and writers in the classroom and/or in the world outside of the classroom, living and dead. In this process she also facilitated their connecting to one another through shared experience, memories, and collaboratively unearthed knowledge, and all kinds of creations including observations, descriptions, scale models, jokes, and vocabulary words, both standard and invented.

Through my participant-observations of Judith Davis I reasoned that, at its best, elementary education directed by powerfully alive teachers nurtured the delight of children in their visceral connections to earth and body. These connections were fed by exploration, care and imagination directed at people, plants and animals, preparation of foods and model shelters, and the general use of diverse art, writing, and measuring materials to document, imagine, remember, and critique experience both inside and outside of school. Text of all kinds provided the context of multiple perspectives on the wider world and its history, responding to or preceding and helping to shape that which was generated in the classroom.

Regarding my emerging conception of parallel practices for teacher education, I reasoned that when the process functions at its worst, teachers who are cut off from their own joy and wonder would take comfort in a standards and test-driven bureaucratic system that eliminated messes, emotions, and attention for sticky social contradictions. Philosopher Sara Ruddick was certainly not alone in tracing the roots of misogyny, a weddedness to the rational and an inability to tolerate difference to inappropriate and/or excessive constraints placed on the developing embodied spirits of children in the service of socialization to an oppressive culture (pp. 131–32).

The implications for teacher education, then, were clear. Teacher educators needed to nurture the capacity for joy and wonder in aspiring teachers. We needed to invite into our own classrooms at the university both messy materials and messy social contradictions. We needed to take time to study critical text, but in a context that left space for playing out the socially reconstructive potential in what we came to understand.

With regard to the use of socially critical text, I have found most critical theory lacking in joy and wonder and remarkably flat with regard to the potentially compelling stickiness of social contradictions. Without the projection of much empathy for the now grown-up excessively constrained embodied spirits of all of us, and certainly the many who joined the teaching profession, critical theorists are typically positioned in their own writings to be the voices of reason and high consciousness in progressive educational foundations courses. Here, they illuminate both the social construction through their previous schooling of the severely limiting attitudes of many who become teachers, and also the mechanisms by which these same teachers and prospective teachers are likely to perpetuate the construction of attitudes like their own in public schools.

They explain how the investment of teachers and administrators in white dominant cultural norms helps reproduce both academic and social schooling practices that justify the power inequities of the economic and political status quo. They describe the initial assumption of some of the people who are now my students that what they can accomplish as teachers is related to making things better for children by rescuing them individually from the limitations of what Maxine Greene (in a benign context) citing the philosopher Charles Taylor,[1] calls their "situatedness." Critical theorists correctly note the absence of a transformative vision of schools as centers for community and aesthetic renewal and families as potential allies in the project of identifying children's needs, strengths, cultural resources, and interests.

Yet neither their analysis nor the analysis of feminist post-structuralists typically transfers well through assigned reading and the usual laissez-faire classroom discussion to those of our students who did not enter the program with a radical political critique. Resistance to the ideas based on both unfamiliarity with the arguments and investment in white and/or class privilege is bolstered by the tendency of the writers to avoid discussion of the legitimate and useful aspects of my students' attraction to teaching children. There is a notable absence of any invitation to prospective and practicing educators to help shape a discourse that might be emancipatory for them as well as the children they teach. Rather, many students feel talked about and talked at in what I join them in characterizing as unnecessarily convoluted language. It is ironic that this language excludes readers who have not had the privilege of a specific type of education, readily identified as elitist, particularly by lower-middle-class/working-class students. Most unfortunately, inaccessible language typically characterizes as well the feminist and feminist post-structuralist critiques of critical theory which might otherwise provide openings for elementary education students, the vast majority of whom are female.

A further problem is that elementary education students in school and community internships, where the children are present every minute and decisions about how to respond need to be made constantly, will find much reinforcement for their growing mistrust of theory. The popular assumption that what is theoretical stands in opposition to what is pragmatic, and *what children can handle is the pragmatic*, can further propel an anti-intellectual orientation that leads to multicultural education beginning and ending with cooking ethnic dishes, flag making, and annual international fairs. Racism and classism are not only uncontested in such environments, the words themselves are literally taboo.

So the stakes involved in the effectiveness of the critical literature we use in elementary teacher education are high; it's not that the interpretations of critical theorists and feminist post-structuralists are wrong; it's that because they often fail to connect on a *visceral* level with their readers, they, in John Dewey's words "purvey cynicism." The words are decontextualized from the hearts and souls of most of the specific individuals who are drawn to elementary education; they fail to call up the activist impulse that will save our students from collusion with the typical school culture where, "accommodations come too easily" (Greene, 1988).

I can best illustrate this problem by offering a critique of a reading that I continue to use with my students despite what I perceive as its shortcomings. Elizabeth Ellsworth's now classic essay, "Why Doesn't This Feel Empowering? Working Through the Repressive Myths of Critical Pedagogy" (1989) does a very fine job of explaining the basic dishonesty of the positioning of the politically "progressive" education professor typically identified as a "critical pedagogue." In order to expose the problematic dependence of the "critical pedagogue" on rationalist judgments about validity, Ellsworth (p. 304) uses African American feminist Barbara Christian's (1987) eloquent assertion that she writes to *save her own life*.[2] By invoking a sense of the proximity to death of aspects of Christian's African American culture (and therefore, of herself), she, Christian, moves us to understand the compelling quality of her words about the work of the culture's women writers. But Ellsworth clarifies that there is no space for such intellectual affirmative action in liberal rationalist discourse; therefore the teaching of different perspectives on any social issue even by "critical pedagogues" will always militate against a fair hearing for the perspective of a marginalized group. When the voices of the marginalized are judged against the voices that have continually reverberated within the margins, rational judgments about value will be biased toward those historically reverberating voices that originally *voiced* the value of the liberal rationalist tradition!

Ellsworth draws an analogy between the positioning of Barbara Christian's words and the words written by the Minority Student Coalition on her own Madison campus. (Her course, C&I 607, Media and Anti-Racist Pedagogies, which is the subject of her article, emerged from the response of this coalition to increasing incidents of racism both on campus and in the Madison community.) She carries us with her in the analogy and uses it later to validate her recognition of the need for speak-outs by students around their own historically misrepresented differences in any future courses like her own. Indeed I have borrowed this strategy for use in my own courses. (A young blond female student demands we assume a high level of intelligence on her part when we speak to her, an Armenian male requires that we recognize the persecution of his people as a genocide, an African American woman requires white feminists to make a commitment to face their own racism before they ask her to speak out on the sexism of her brothers.)

But near the conclusion of Ellsworth's article, she and I part company: When her colleague, Albert Selvin, asserts that "as a White man/boy [he] was not allowed to be anything but cut off from the earth and the body,"[3] the tragedy he describes is lost in the positioning of his comments. Ellsworth contextualizes his words in a discussion of "the mythical norm deployed for the purpose of setting the standard of humanness against which Others are defined and assigned privilege and limitations." Selvin is closer to that norm which is "young, white, heterosexual, Christian, able-bodied, thin, middle-class, English-speaking, and male." No matter what Ellsworth says about the need to contextualize, as opposed to relativize specific experiences of oppression, the reader is supposed to see Selvin, and by extension Selvin's words, as less compelling than those of Barbara Christian or the Minority Student Coalition.

The problem is that I see my colleagues, myself, my students and even Ellsworth's students as identified with Selvin, and we will be the teachers of Barbara Christian's children and grandchildren. There is a lack of attention in Ellsworth's argument to the reality that rationalist discourses will continue to marginalize Others as long as men like Selvin and all the rest of us, male and female, growing up in a bureaucratized, de-spiritualized, and passive (except in relation to consumption) culture are cut off from the resources with which to begin collaborative construction of the curriculum of our own lives. Those resources are the *visceral* stuff of human life, the connective tissue inside and between us, and the mud on which we walk, the precisely appropriate *foundations* for quality elementary education.

Neither Ellsworth nor other feminist post-structuralists suggest that the conception of our white middle-class students as *privileged* comes out of its own necessarily limited discourse; yet privileges are often dispensed in the form of privileged socialization, socialization that frequently has as its goal eliminating the possibility that its recipients will choose to do physical work (except doctoring) or *dirty* work. It is ironic that critical theorists and feminist post-structuralists who wish to undermine Euro-centrism continue to marginalize conceptions of higher consciousness rooted in awareness of body and earth that have traditionally prevailed in much of the non-Western world. In the thinking of yoga, for example, privileges with regard to access to power and material wealth are viewed as corrupting influences on the mind, body, and spirit. And interestingly, the path to personal happiness and spiritual enlightenment is conceptualized as beginning with body consciousness and a closeness to nature, two, again, precisely appropriate *foundations* for quality elementary education.

Such discourses open us to another possibility denied in most of the critical, even the social reconstructionist scholarship in our field: that human beings are necessarily limited creatures. Although we have long accepted the partial nature of what each individually situated one of us can know, and therefore reasonably be expected to act on, this awareness has never translated into an understanding of why social justice seekers are often disappointed. Perhaps we might want to consider a curriculum for schooling that begins with an awareness of realistic human limitation, captured by both Salman Rushdie and six-year-old J. in their characters, the Misters Butt. We might take seriously Sara Ruddick's acknowledgment of the predictable fascination and ambivalence we all carry about being developing spirits encased in bodies (that will die). There are certainly many uses for the empathy and energy such an approach might make available for the complex and unpredictable directions to which our work as social justice–focused teachers will propel us.

The work now required of elementary educators includes the

same "classroom practice of the unknowable," the same complex provision of "support [for] students/[teacher] in the never-ending *moving about"* Ellsworth proposes for social-justice–seeking professors.[4] Yet our students, who are or will be teachers, only rarely come to us with the same explicit commitments as those who self-selected for Ellsworth's Media and Anti-Racist Pedagogies course at Madison.

The argument in Ellsworth's otherwise wonderful article remains captive to the rationalist discourses that the activist work pursued by herself and her students begins to undermine. Without attention to a discourse of the human spirit the best-intentioned educational researchers cannot offer compelling motivation to pursue social justice for students and teachers whose lives have been generally constrained by dominant culture norms and who, therefore, have had little experience with the richness of living consciously in the many and often conflicting ethnic, geographic, racial, social class, and gender identities they might claim or reclaim.

This book begins with the use of a citation from John Dewey to establish such a non-dogmatic discourse of the human spirit. In Chapter 1 the implications for such a discourse on activity in the teacher education classroom are explored. Chapter 2 further develops the connection between such a discourse and the study of social reconstructionist text in the teacher education classroom. Chapter 3 features a day-in-the-life journey into two adjoining elementary classrooms where teachers and children enact this non-dogmatic discourse of the human spirit. The curriculum of the classrooms that are the subject of this chapter resonates with the themes of the social reconstructionist teacher education classrooms featured in the first two and last two chapters; this focus on the elementary classroom is purposefully positioned to occupy the center of the book. Chapter 4 connects the teacher educator's life in her own community with the preparation for activism she offers her students, suggesting the possibility of a "dialectic of freedom" (Greene, 1988) operating from both directions, from the social reconstructionist teacher education classroom to the community, and from the community back to the process of educating teachers. And finally, Chapter 5 begins to explore my highest goals for this work, *social action as curriculum* for the communities encompassing both the teacher education and the elementary school classrooms.

The reader needs to be aware that my ideas have been shaped in courses that serve the needs of a variety of education students; although my interpretations are focused on implications for elementary teacher education, I teach in a small department where a number of my courses are available to secondary teachers and others in the community as well. Although the largest share of my energies go toward the development of our pre-professional master's programs in elementary education, I do have some already certified practicing elementary teachers in some of my classes. Also, I regularly teach Social and Philosophical Issues in Education in our practitioner-oriented doctoral program, where student response to our work together influences my thinking as well.

Chapter One
The Author Re-evaluates Her Earliest Elementary Teaching Model in the Service of Prizing the Stuff of John Dewey's "Human Life":
How a Conception of "Wholeness of Labor" Might Generate Parallel Practices for Elementary Curriculum and Teacher Education Work

> Thus the question of integration of mind-body in action is the most practical of all questions we can ask of our civilization. It is not just a speculative question, it is a demand—a demand that the labor of multitudes now too predominantly physical in character be inspirited by purpose and emotion and informed by knowledge and understanding. It is a demand that what now pass for highly intellectual and spiritual functions shall be integrated with the ultimate conditions and means of all achievement, namely the physical, and thereby accomplish something beyond themselves. Until this integration is effected in the only place where it can be carried out, in action itself, we shall continue to live in a society in which a soulless and heartless materialism is compensated for by soulful but futile idealism and spiritualism. (Dewey in Alexander, 1932)[1]

> The division in question is so deep-seated that it has affected even our language. We have no word by which to name mind-body in a unified wholeness of operation. For if we said "human life" few would recognize that it is precisely the unity of mind and body in action to which we were referring. (Dewey, 1928)[2]

I offer these citations from John Dewey as introduction to an autobiographically based exploration of the parallel practice implications for social justice–focused teacher education in a specific interpretation of the work of one multi-age primary classroom teacher, Judith Davis. Judith Davis was the rural upstate New York cooperating teacher with whom I student taught in 1972 and to whom I returned eighteen years later (in 1990) in order to interpret her primary literacy curriculum for my dissertation. Dewey's words capture my most recent understanding of the importance of Judith Davis's curriculum-making in her primary classroom, an approach that affected all of my subsequent work related to human growth in community, including my own critical literacy work with children and young adults, and for the past seven years, my teaching in social justice–focused teacher education.

By now, I think it's become clearer to many of us who see ourselves as "progressives" or "reformers" in teacher education that the removal of obstacles in the way of achieving social equity in schools might require attention to what kind of life, both collective and individual, we want social equity to make possible. We have reached a historical moment when the rapid corporatization of meaning-making lends particular urgency to the work of recovering for our teacher education students and the children they will teach a compelling conception of healthy human life that the phenomenon of oppression distorts. Otherwise we collude with the current national trend of shaping into competitive test-takers the children our students will teach, the future passive consumers of the "soulless" global marketplace characterized by Dewey above. Or we turn against public education completely, substituting progressive theorizing about the replication of social inequity in schools for the much harder work of forging theory-practice connections with our students, and purveying cynicism through our "futile idealism."

Until my discovery of the specific and lesser-known Dewey lectures from which the above citations are selected, it was difficult to directly share with my students the valuable lessons about making sense of life with children that I learned from Judith Davis and from other teachers who modeled similar practices. The valuable conception "maternal thinking" I borrowed from feminist philosopher Sara Ruddick in an effort to capture the spirit of Judith Davis's practices already assumed a rich knowledge base about curriculum-making that many of my students did not have. Ruddick's work also provoked the charge of "maternal essentialism" and was therefore dismissed as sexist by a number of my students, colleagues, and prospective publishers. My defense of her work echoed her own: that women have historically done this work and were therefore in the best position to assess and internalize its lessons. Yet these discussions drained valuable time from classes in which we needed to enact the practice implications of the theory we studied. Although doctoral students and sometimes master's students investigating their own practices in their action research projects at the end of our program appreciated her work, it proved too subtle and complex for courses that were not primarily about curriculum theorizing.

The discovery of these Dewey citations, however, has helped me forge a more direct translation of Ruddick's feminist philosophy into supports for social reconstructionist curriculum-making, building on her theme of valuing and reclaiming connections. (See Chapter 3.) It also helps me identify the potentially feminist spark in Dewey's own work. I can re-interpret for myself and my students what my most effective teacher did that offered me an initial powerful orientation to this work: Judith Davis modeled a basis for elementary curriculum in the reversal of the division of labor's artificial separation of *thinking* work and *doing* work. Further, this curriculum was represented in her classroom as natural: the stuff of "human life" that Dewey equates (above) with "mind-body in wholeness of operation" and I interpret as the individual human being's refusal to internalize the division of labor as "normal." Expressed positively, her curriculum might be interpreted as orienting children to participation in a social life and intellectual life consonant with the "wholeness of labor" (my words).

What has been most significant in the pursuit of this thinking relative to my teaching is the power of the non-dogmatic, spiritual conception "wholeness of labor." It appears to offer my students an entry point for the radical political implications of Dewey's famous curriculum work, best exemplified in *The School and Society The Child and the Curriculum,* which they study in our program. Although they typically have been inspired by both the activity-orientation of Dewey's elementary curriculum and by the emphasis on children's interests as a starting point for curriculum-making, the connections between that curriculum and the pursuit of social and economic democracy have remained abstract. But Dewey's thinking as conveyed in the above citations, which clearly links personal empowerment to the body's inextricable connections with the mind, has radical and global political implications.

This focus on "wholeness of labor" has begun to reshape my thinking about appropriate curriculum for social justice–focused teacher education. Relative to the content of this chapter, Judith Davis's seamless integration of thinking work and doing work has inspired in me an appreciation for how my own curriculum in social justice–focused teacher education has been evolving a "parallel practices" theme; increasingly, I require of myself not only that my work with the students integrates critical social foundations knowledge with the process of developing appropriate curriculum for socially diverse elementary classrooms, but also that it replicates in spirit and content Dewey's "human life," "mind-body in wholeness of operation" for classroom life both in elementary schools and in teacher education.

In this chapter I want to construct as parallel practices my own curriculum-making at present in our social justice–focused master's program in elementary education at Binghamton University with certain aspects of Judith Davis's curriculum-making from my work with her as both student teacher and dissertation researcher. It is Dewey's "mind-body in wholeness of operation" as it exemplifies the "wholeness of labor" that constitutes these "parallel practices" in our work; my hope is that the multiple commonalities in the two tiers of work will inspire my readers to develop the many possible curricular implications we have not thought of yet in Dewey's plea for inspiriting action and, conversely, for purposeful action in response to our intellectual and spiritual awarenesses.

A brief vignette from my student teaching experience

Philip Wexler's call to resacralize ordinary life for public education (1996) evoked my experience student teaching in Judith Davis's classroom in 1972 when people were not yet speaking in terms of "whole language," even in New Zealand, but opposition to the war in Vietnam and the movements that encompassed it or were empowered by it had popularized a radical social critique that influenced public schooling. Specifically, Lillian Weber's conception of "open education" was shaping the practices of a number of teachers in the primary building of the upstate New York rural school district where Judith Davis taught.

Though not herself politically radical, Judith Davis was all about the search for "holy sparks"[3] of meaning in a material world where things were not fair, constantly telling stories that led to theorizing about life, its peculiar positive surprises, beauty, and injustices as well as our capacity to have an impact on it, and encouraging the children to do the same, whether they could write the words or not. I loved what she modeled; it came naturally to me to sit down with one of the children from a migrant family,[4] up from a small town in Florida until the apple crop was picked, and create what was then called a language experience story: asking the child if she wanted me to write down her story about some aspect of the trip up from down South, being in our school for only two-and-a-half months while living at the camp, and going home again. I would write every word the child said, and we'd share the story in group meeting where the other kids, working class, poor, and middle class in about equal numbers, were impressed with how you could live in a camp where lots of people ate and played and worked very closely together and even a second grader could know so much about what apples were worth and the best techniques for picking the different kinds. There would always be a few children who couldn't get close enough to the story chart paper in group meeting. They had to get their fingers on certain words, because the encoding of meaning in them was compelling in a physical way; they had to touch the words, often smudging that bright white paper, pointing out how many times "apple" appeared.

I remember that early on in my student teaching after sharing one of these stories, we gave every child a choice of light green or light yellow construction paper shaped like a halved apple and the children were asked to illustrate and/or write their own story based on any memory they had involving apples. And while they were doing this, Judith Davis huddled with me in a corner and pointed out how little time there was to teach the migrant kids to read and how important it was that we follow up on those language experience stories with some intensive decoding skills. She showed me a box of cards called "Glass Analysis" that grouped words together in families based on vowel sounds and asked if I'd like to spend fifteen minutes or so every early morning with four children, two of them from migrant families and two of them from long-term white residents with grandparents in the town; she said she was sure these four would be helped by this work.

I continued to take dictations of fascinating stories from these children and all of the children and to share them with the whole group during meeting time; and every day we also worked on identifying the cards of a different word family in between the science experiments in which nylon stockings rubbed with plastic bags filled up like real legs from static electricity and the trips outside to collect bark and sticks for the dioramas of Iroquois longhouse life and the making of applesauce. We grabbed time in between these real "human life" experiences that no child could miss in order to learn the decoding tricks that were practice for reading, according to both Judith Davis and Joy Moss, the marvelous teacher of the literacy class I was taking at the University of Rochester simultaneous with student teaching. The key was to find out who needed how much practice and to be clear that such practice never substituted for the more visceral stuff of classroom life where you used reading and writing to capture and learn more about what you discovered, and to dictate, write, or read real and imaginative stories about life to inspire you to see possibilities you might not have thought of yet.

Gradually, the children in my first group of four were able to read significant portions of their dictated stories during group meetings and I remember now, almost thirty years later in this era of unprecedented and wrong-headed focus on standards and testing, that three of them, including both of the children from migrant families, tested "on level" before all of the migrant workers and their children left to pick oranges down South in the middle of November.

Like Dewey's labschool, that classroom modeled the real-life collaboration necessitated by the mutual interdependence of a pre-industrial rural community; everybody needed to be useful all the time: there were often messes to clean up and you couldn't rely on immediate adult direction: occasionally somebody's mother was standing in the doorway confiding to Judith Davis about her worries focused on an older child; there was hair to pull behind somebody's ear so it wouldn't get in the applesauce pot, children constantly huddled close together getting a good look at a box of antique fish hooks or a captioned picture from a history or natural science text Judith Davis had brought in response to a child's query from the day before, and a continual search for the pencils and markers (that should have been on the science table) so you could write down what you noticed or figured out, and of course a never-ending request of one another for words.

And then there was the consciousness of the material world out there where some kids "were not going to make it" if they didn't have "the skills to succeed." Those were Judith Davis's words voiced right in front of the children; she would never have said "dominant culture skills" or "the codes of the culture of power" or "cultural capital," but that's what she meant. It did not interrupt the visceral feel of the classroom, because her concerns were so real, and the children took them up as such, sometimes the whole class moving aside the clay and bark and paint for partnered drills of math facts, or work on word families, or occasionally handwriting practice. There was a lot of laughter and occasional yelling; Judith Davis sometimes required a little too much cooperation and judgment for eight-year-olds, it seemed to me, and she could get pretty harsh when her expectations were disappointed, but her behavior was consistent with the tone in which she told them repeatedly that "life was not a Disney cartoon."

"Human life" and activism

Interestingly, many of the teachers involved in the development of the Lillian Weber–inspired "integrated day" primary program modeled in Judith Davis's practices became directly involved with the migrant community as political advocates and activists. One became a founder of a local anti-racism coalition, one, still a close friend, became a liaison person who negotiated with local growers around migrant worker rights, and one wrote the grant that paid me a summer salary to write and produce plays with young people in four different migrant communities.

I was also formally hired as a teacher in that school beginning spring term of my student teaching year, but when I left three-and-a-half years later, initially to participate in Lillian Weber's Summer Immersion Experience in Open Education at City College in New York, I became a non-violent radical political activist. And at the risk of oversimplification, I want to say that it was the desire to preserve the "human life" modeled in Judith Davis's classroom that had its brilliance affirmed at Lillian Weber's Workshop Center, the way both environments projected an understanding of the sacredness of the project of human growth, that compelled me toward the activism that has been a part of my life since.

In studying two consecutive springs worth of writing workshop in Judith Davis's classroom for my dissertation eighteen years after student teaching with her, three themes emerged continually in the talk I studied, which she orchestrated during the "mini-lessons" that preceded the children's individual writing block: a valuing of the visceral (of the sacred place of the body, and especially the body's association with movement, food, sex, and death in all of our lives); an appreciation of humor, used most notably for its ability both to help bridge painful social contradictions and illuminate the struggles of growing up human as they announced themselves in this socially diverse environment; and a view of history as the collectivity of stories about how people acted on and influenced the circumstances of their lives, including the children's lives in this classroom. There was attention to the stories of the children and of their families and communities that included the stories of those no longer living, all of them open to multiple interpretations. This view of history then determined that words, both conventional and invented, existed to facilitate connection and purposeful action between and among our storied lives, including the lives of those not represented in this particular already extended classroom community. Words could motivate or make possible new action; thus they generated new history.

Relevance of "human life" for my students

These are themes I present to my teacher education students, contextualized now in two different bodies of John Dewey's thinking, but unified by his opposition to the division of labor—by an identification of "human life" with what I call "wholeness of labor." I explicitly connect this conception with the philosophy of Maxine Greene, the contemporary curriculum work of teachers associated with Rethinking Schools like Linda Christensen (2000) and accessible revisionist historians like James Loewen (1995). Without patronizing my students, I want to say that many talented elementary education students come to this work primarily from their hearts, often with intellectual curiosity that has not been appropriately developed in their own typically traditional formal educational experience. My experience of the past eight years in teacher education has taught me that such students can become significantly educated both intellectually and politically if our teaching values the body, heart and mind, Dewey's "mind-body," and lends credibility to a conception of a "human spirit" that grows in proportion with opportunities to engage in what Dewey calls in this same body of thinking, "purposeful action."

In many cases, our students' access to their own "mind-body" has been short-circuited; as Dewey intimates, they have absorbed from the wider culture a conception of themselves as passive consumers of both conventional commodities and of knowledge as commodity. Yet the attachment to children that has typically propelled them into this work is often the key to their willingness to reevaluate their own formal and informal educational experience. I have observed that their ability to identify with the propensity of children to favor action and activist responses to their own observations and realizations (knowledge) has been far less compromised. My students are quick to appreciate the extent to which Dewey's "human life" is typically suppressed in school, where classrooms like Judith Davis's are rare.

The pinchpot lesson

The origins and rationale for the use of this lesson with my current teacher education students in our social justice–focused elementary master's program at Binghamton University bears explanation. I first conceived of it as a potentially important piece of curriculum for all ages while reading an assigned book that I am unfortunately now unable to locate or identify for a study group I attended as a member of the short-lived Rochester Progressive Movement in the late 1970s. The particular chapter of interest was about early and ancient history, and I believe the book's Marxist author was making the point that all technological "advances" have the potential to exacerbate power imbalances in the human communities in which they are developed or introduced. My memory is that the author used the clay pot as an example. Specifically, I remembered having an "aha" moment when this author pointed out that the container introduced the potential to hoard food.

This memory came back to me one evening a few years ago when I was trying to conceive of an activity that would demonstrate for my students what my new conception, "wholeness of labor" might feel like. If Dewey was correct that the division of labor was antithetical to humanness, and the division of labor was a cultural norm for myself and my students, then how could we *know* the disempowerment that existed for us only as a political argument? Another complication was the reality that many of my students felt personally invested in the thinking pole of the division of labor and, therefore, might experience Dewey's opposition to it as against their own interests. I wanted them in particular to get some intimation of a possible sacrifice on the part of those defined as "cultured" in this inhumane social arrangement. It occurred to me that we needed to simulate in class the kind of thoughtful, socially aware "making" that Dewey contended was precisely what most human beings want to do.

I asked my students to imagine themselves as an early human community in which "the container" had just been discovered. I passed around two ten-pound blocks of clay along with a wire for cutting individual portions, purposely organizing the activity so that collective distribution of the materials required became part of the process of this lesson. I offered the following direction: we were going to build individual pinchpots with the clay provided while collectively brainstorming the "positive" and "negative" effects on our early community's evolving culture of the advent (or emergence) of the container.

Most of the students were delighted to be doing something with their hands outside of an art class. I observed that many of them experienced the same joy I do in cutting clay with a wire; for students who had never done this before there was visceral pleasure in the evenness with which the blocks separated and a fascination with the now-visible inside texture of the clay. Some enjoyed the straight angles so much that they asked if "[it had] to be a pot? Couldn't it be rectangular?" Soon there was dialogue about comparative approaches to container-making; some pursued slab-building, others the pinch method; many wound coils; one student wove a tight basket with thin long flat strips of clay. Memories were voiced about kindergarten clay projects: a precious snowman lost in a kiln, pride in a hand impression, the rush to finish a pot before the bell, to find a safe place to put it to make sure it wouldn't get wrecked.

K. in my Social Action as Curriculum course commented at about this point in the lesson, "But we were never asked to make any association with early people, or with people who make pots now for a living and/or as art. It was just clay time." S. remembered making pots associated with the study of Native Americans. A fascinating conversation ensued, linked to their recent reading of the

Loewen book, *Lies My Teacher Told Me* (1995). Two students, B. and N., supported one another in the argument that introducing pots to children only in connection with Native Americans kept both subjects, "Native Americans" and "pots" in the category "primitive people and things." In this class I recommended that the students read (and promised to bring to our next meeting a copy of the book) *Through Indian Eyes* (Slapin and Seale, 1992), an annotated bibliography of children's literature about native Americans, pointing out that the book suggested that an analogous kind of categorizing (analogous to B. and N.'s category "primitive") as "animal-like" could happen when children were introduced to nature primarily through study of Native Americans.

I also used my own reference to the book as a teachable moment, pointing out that all of us who conceived of ourselves as learners, adults and children alike, were strongly reinforced by the offer of a book that connected with a thoughtful comment, observation, or interest we had voiced. I urged them to introduce books and other resources into their classrooms in response to the comments of individual children, and to at least sometimes allow the focus of the whole-class curriculum to spiral from these spontaneously introduced resources.

After about five minutes of this informal discussion I drew attention to the chart paper set up to record responses to my original inquiry; I suggested they brainstorm first in small groups while building their pots and then report back to the whole group at which time I'd do the actual recording of responses on the paper so they could continue pot-building. Many students were invested in creating beautiful pots, including experimentation with handles and surface texture. In both experiences of this lesson in my curriculum courses, at least one student asked if we could leave time to show one another our finished products. The request provided another teachable moment around the importance of attractively displaying people's/children's work, and the inspiration toward higher quality work provided by such displays. In one of these experiences we not only shared our work at the end of class but also made suggestions about how it could have been formally displayed in a classroom museum, brainstorming the unit topics in which the pot display might have been contextualized. L. shared her observation that the children from her classroom internship experience particularly loved writing for such purposes and that the classroom teacher was able to help them appreciate the difference in attention to presentation required for personal journaling versus captioning for the classroom's "public" museum.

> Directions: You are an early human community which has just discovered or uncovered or developed the first container known to your group. Predict any possible positive and negative effects on your community of the introduction of this new technology.

Discussion in the small groups was consistently lively; in my multiculturalism course one group later brought to the whole class their argument about whether "more leisure time because you needed less food-gathering" was necessarily positive. A student in that group argued that leisure time is what caused our current entertainment culture, leading to kids in schools expecting constant entertainment from us, their teachers: hence, what we were learning to provide in this class! Everybody laughed. Another countered, But isn't that what we develop new technology for—to have more leisure time? R. called out, "Yeah, we all know how much leisure time the computer has given us!" General laughter again. I made a note to bring to the next class multiple copies of the most recent edition of an Ithaca free monthly literary arts newspaper that featured an article by a Cornell professor questioning the value of computers and based on the very same point about time raised by R.

In that particular class most of the students wanted to leave "the capacity to store food" in the positive column, but a consensus was reached that I "decenter" it in its column on the chart paper, allowing it to occupy a space mostly in the positive, but partly in the negative column. After that we placed "diseases caused by food storage" solidly in the negative. "Development of creative arts and aesthetic consciousness" was placed in the positive column, and not decentered, even though one student raised the issue of the potential for fashion and decorative arts to become a negative social force. In two classes we had hilarious conversations about whether "more sexual activity" was a logical consequence of "food storage capacity," and then, if "more sexual activity" was positive or negative!

Interestingly, in all four experiences nobody voiced "possible hoarding of food or water" before I did, even though three classes included "wars" as a negative effect. A number of students made it clear that they identified with C., who called out, "I was about to say that, but I thought it sounded too negative." In the discussion that followed I asked the students to consider the implications of our not wanting to voice a "negative" human social behavior like "hoarding food." E., having just completed the Loewen book, suggested a connection with Loewen's argument; we were refusing to verbalize what we, as human beings, really do. "War is more amorphous, but hoarding food—somebody clearly *starts* that. We can acknowledge that we human beings collectively cause wars, but nobody wants to be an individual hoarder of food. And that's why social studies education is so boring," she added.

In different classes the wrestling with this issue of food hoarding has taken different forms. In one class a student raised the point that it's not everybody who hoards food, only the people and nations with the power to do so. Twice we have been able to explore the arbitrariness of national borders in the context of this discussion. And in both curriculum classes students had an immediate association with a particular unit on local milk production explored in some detail by teacher Julia Weber Gordon in *My Country School Diary*[5] (1946), which we had just read in conjunction with the Dewey text. M. voiced a frustration with which I completely identified: how, in the current historical era, could a classroom teacher facilitate the successful intervention of her children in the issue of irrational distribution of food in their geographic region, comparable to the way Julia Weber Gordon was able to involve her students in empowering the local milk cooperative in 1937? (pp. 125–42).

Interestingly, during the term following the above class discussion, a student in my Social Action as Curriculum course who had grown up on a dairy farm asked and tried to answer a very similar question. Although he eventually changed his project (the road-blocks in the way of his inquiry were more administrative than political), he actually did succeed in bringing together a group of young students from a Future Farmers of America club and a group of local farmers organizing politically for more rational policy governing dairy farming at the national and state levels.

The classroom teaching experiences described above have moved me to consider taking a more active role in supporting students to investigate such social justice questions, perhaps by focusing their final curriculum projects on a unit plan that emerges from the particularly "live" issues raised in class. Such an approach, a concerted effort to tie assignments to explorations of obvious collective interest and compelling importance for future social justice–focused teachers might also meet another need. It would offer me an alternative to subtle silencing of students like T., who earnestly voice what a number of others are thinking when issues related to privilege, like "food hoarding" arise: "But the United States is always shipping food to starving countries." Social Action as Curriculum is beginning to provide a forum for investigating the multiple perspectives on social issues, even on "knowledge," that regularly arise in class, a significant development given that exploration of multiple perspectives is the precisely appropriate foundation for the social studies curriculum of their own future classrooms. In the curriculum course, I am moving toward providing opportunity for a final curriculum project that includes the provision for collective work in a group with diverse knowledge bases and perspectives, so that a student like S., who responded to T.'s assertion that "U.S. and European-based multinationals graze cattle on land that peasants can't use to grow crops; that's one reason why people starve," might end up cooperating with T. on this assignment.

Parallel practices

The conversation generated by and during the pinchpot lesson is rooted in the same visceral themes that emerged in my study of Judith Davis's classroom. There is even the reliance on humor and the construction of a feeling of safety out of which emerges deeper consideration of social equity issues. Future curriculum is propelled out of conversation; future study of specific text is determined on an as-needed as-relevant basis, as Dewey intimated and both Julia Weber Gordon and Judith Davis modeled as a regular practice. There is the sense that active response to thinking that emerges as talk is "natural"; it is, after all, what Dewey defines as "human life." And students internalize "whole language" thinking at a deeper level; they see that they themselves can use written language in order to negotiate meanings with potential impact on their own communities.

Ironically, it is the curriculum course that tends to be so packed with texts and ideas we feel compelled to "cover" that it is challenging to pursue the leads introduced by student talk and writing. Yet, with my intention to model parallel practices, the spiraling of curriculum in class is precisely what I want to be doing. Elementary teacher education students in particular need to appreciate the process of developing rich curricular content in a context where research-based assignments to be pursued outside of class are limited by the appropriate focus of young children in particular on more concrete, immediate, and less academic considerations.

In both Social Action as Curriculum and Foundations of Multiculturalism, I was able to spiral curriculum from the pinchpot lesson in two different directions: for the session of the Social Action class after the pinchpot lesson I collected six copies of Byrd Baylor's children's picture book *The Desert Is Theirs* (1975) and reproduced the book review about it from *Through Indian Eyes*. The students were able to read both the book and the review in their small groups, and also to briefly discuss how they might address in their curriculum with young children the concerns of the Native American reviewer parallel to those that had emerged in our class while still enjoying the book's obvious merits. Sacrificing a whole-group discussion, this spontaneous lesson took about a half an hour. The experience left me considering building such flexibility into the design of the curriculum course, perhaps by eliminating one of our assigned texts.

Re-valuing Dewey

But such speculation has relevance to my rationale for the pinchpot lesson. We, ourselves, and the students we teach are temporally distant from the preindustrial social relations, with their potential for social and economic democracy visible, that Dewey used as model for his labschool (Dewey, 1902/1990). It is very easy for us to romanticize rather than take seriously the implications for our teaching of both the connectedness of family and community members and the "busy-ness" of children's lives around intentional pursuits as portrayed by Dewey, and not only because Dewey sometimes romanticized these relationships and "occupations" himself. I believe we romanticize for a number of reasons: because of our distance from the context of intentionality/purposefulness that was visible in the lives of folks who had some control over the simple means of production that provided their livelihood, because we are so uncertain about the malleability of our current (in some ways gratifying) social construction as largely consuming individualists, and because Dewey's model labschool community did not know the challenges of social and cultural diversity that we and our students currently face. There is tension in the project of building fully inclusive communities, and discussing this tension has been taboo for progressives until relatively recently.

But in these lectures of Dewey's that have gotten scant attention there is the sense that "human life" is what happens when "mind-body" stay integrated. It may well be the case that attention to our personal physical, spiritual and emotional resources, often dismissed by progressives as bourgeois pursuits, would reward us with the necessary stamina, the "wild patience" prescribed by Maxine Greene (p. 135) for all of us involved in educating teachers.

Dewey's later-in-life faith, actually made the most clear in his introduction to F. M. Alexander's *The Use of the Self* (1932) and in his 1938 lectures to the New York Medical Society from which the respective citations that introduce this chapter were drawn, was that the integration of every individual's mind and body in purposeful action, an integration contested by an increasingly corporatized, and therefore, bureaucratized culture, was the hope for building a democratic society. He, himself practiced the Alexander Technique, which he advocated for both in Alexander's book and in these lectures. The Alexander Technique is in fact a system of achieving or reclaiming natural body alignment coordinated with the breath. It shares with yoga the higher spiritual goal of stilling the modifications of the mind. Key in understanding the relevance for social reconstructionist education is Dewey's awareness that these modifications are typically socially constructed. In other words, Dewey, following Alexander, came to believe that the breath was the resource for "mind-body in wholeness of operation"—quite literally the resource for his rich conception of "human life." But the physical body could become constrained in its movements as a result of patterns of internalizing both oppression and personal pain. Such constraints blocked the breath and created a cyclical kind of dysfunction, whereby inefficient breathing further constrained the movement of the body.

Although the conception of human life he articulated here emerged for Dewey out of his own personal commitment to the specific practice of Alexander, the citations make clear that Dewey appreciated these practices for their metaphoric and philosophical direction for education as well. Likewise, my purpose here is not to prescribe either the Alexander Technique or yoga for my readers, much as I value both practices in my own life, but rather, to explore how we might keep Dewey's rich conception of "human life" front and center in elementary school curriculum and in curriculum for social justice–focused teacher education.

Interestingly, in her essay in *Black Looks* (1992), "Revolutionary Black Women," African American social critic, activist, and educator bell hooks emphasized the personal commitment to healing mental and physical pain that would make possible effective social justice–focused movement-building among black women. And Maxine Greene of course recognized the personal responsibility of teachers and their allies to wake up, notice, and act—to seize the "dialectic of freedom" (1988) in order to overcome social obstacles, to join with others toward a perceived common good. For all the complexity of these thinkers, like Dewey, there is a focus on the most basic requirement for those who insist that human beings have agency: take power over your own life even as you strategize with others to build a more just social world.

It's all too easy to back off as individuals into the realm of explanatory theory in this era where those of us who came to teacher education out of a will to end social oppression are not exactly sure what to do. The same is the case for those of our students who live their lives in the victim role relative to classism, racism, and/or sexism, oppressions that appear to shift in their manifestations rather than become any less potent. While social construction theory can help us analyze how we are shaped by the prevailing norms of the cultures in which we live, it doesn't offer much direction for taking responsibility—for what Dewey calls "purposeful action." And the retreat into the head can be particularly devastating for those of us who need to inspire students to create an appropriate curriculum of purposeful action for the elementary school classroom.

For me, the clay in the pinchpot lesson is a more than symbolic striking out against the use of the intellect to avoid engagement with the real stuff of life, which of course does include intellect, as modeled in Judith Davis's classroom. The clay itself invokes the body, reassuring both in its continual breath and its expanding and contracting substance. It is literally elemental. And when my students engage with the clay, I see the most elemental signs of aliveness: non-derisive laughter, the evocation of memories, the beginning of queries that have depth, the intention to create something beautiful, the appeal of purpose.

That this purposefulness which our students typically find so appealing was historically enforced by the need to organize resources for self-preservation is often a startling realization. Most of our

American-born education students equate economics with a capitalist conception of the play of market forces. Thus they have internalized a kind of mystification that allows them to accept the naturalness of manipulation of the availability of resources; many of our students conceive of economic forces from both essentialist and distanced perspectives. They view them as operating "out there," having never been invited to think about how they got "out there."

In the pinchpot lesson, students get an intimation of what their usual removal both from the visceral aspects of production and from the processes of local democracy as Dewey envisioned it (1902/1990, pp. 10–14) removes them *from*—possibly an intimation of what it might be like to decide—along with the people in our communities, what we actually need and want, and how and under what circumstances to create and distribute it. Dewey intimates that this kind of thinking, the thinking about creativity, production, sensible distribution, and preservation of resources, is precisely what the majority of thinking human beings who are not-primarily-intellectuals want to think about and are good at thinking about.

My experience has been that our students, in fact, relate very strongly to this conception of human intelligence and can come to appreciate how their own intelligence is short-circuited in this passive consumerist culture that effectively manages them. Related, students who are practicing teachers have made the connection with the managed curriculum they are encouraged—and in the current climate of high-stakes standards and testing—sometimes forced—to teach.

Therefore, the rationale for this lesson includes the expansion of the students' capacity to think about the development of technology as always evoking social contradictions, and therefore, requiring the kind of thinking and dialogue that is both part of—and leads to—Dewey's "purposeful action." Perhaps of particular importance is the realization that the emergence of any new technological development provides the most promising site for truly democratic discourse precisely because it introduces the potential for exacerbation of power imbalances in any social grouping in which it emerges.

Because the pinchpot activity opens us to exploration of the relationship between individual ownership of proportionally greater amounts of social wealth and resulting power imbalances in the society, it offers an excellent context for understanding the functioning of dominant culture, the culture that determines what Judith Davis named for the children "the skills to succeed." As soon as students note that some "early people" would figure out that having disproportionately more pots could lead to that group's control of the community food supply, they understand how ideology can emerge to justify undemocratic practices in a community. Invoking Maxine Greene's conception of the "dialectic of freedom," we can make the connections between "what becomes thinkable" socially and the history of distribution of the material/technological developments so central to Dewey's curriculum for the elementary school classroom.

Dewey was never very effective at describing clearly the value of what he called "occupations," outside of the basic understanding that doing and making appealed to children's interests. He naively overestimated the positive potential of technology. And when he worked at distancing himself from the advocates of pure child-centeredness, challenging more forcefully what he saw as the misguided polarization of child and curriculum, few practitioners had the experience to understand his critique. But students involved in such doing and making (of the pinchpots) with a connection provided to the democratic discourse Dewey envisioned as socially necessary in challenging the division of labor (pp. 22–29) report finding their critical thinking capacities awakened; further, the Dewey curriculum becomes understandable, sometimes for the first time.

Our students have an advantage over us in that they are or will be teaching very young people who have not internalized to the extent we (and our students) have the dominant culture's message that the work of the mind is separate from the work of the body. Many young children still believe that they can learn from their own experience and their own observations. We in teacher education, however, must re-teach that truth to our students with methods intended for people who are not primarily interested in social theory, even theory that helps to explain the very personal limitations that confound them as they begin teaching in diverse classrooms and facing children who see the world differently than they do.

According to Dewey, the capacity to make connections begins with restoration of the elemental one between mind and body. We can begin that process in our classes with provision of the very concrete materials like clay that can be molded, shaped by us for service in the world. Then we can begin the dialogue obscured by the information age of the global economy by asking: what do people really need, how should such things be produced and distributed, what would a fair reward structure look like, how can we make use of the fact about ourselves that Dewey and Judith Davis understood? We want to be able to think about what we are doing; we want to do what makes sense to us in the context of living in community with others who have equally worthy wants (pp. 27–28). There is no dialogue more compelling to young people; thus such dialogue presents the perfect "parallel practices" opportunity for the teaching of adults who will teach children.

Chapter Two
Using Classic Social Reconstructionist Text in Elementary Teacher Education:
Study Guides and Lesson Plans to Move Prospective Elementary Educators Beyond Laissez-Faire Discussion Toward a Commitment to Social Justice

The purpose of this chapter is to present an orientation to the use of study guides and lesson plans/assignments that I believe is especially suited to challenging elementary education students and teachers with regard to their ability to think critically about both broader social issues and their own acquisition of knowledge. I began developing these lesson plans/assignments in general education courses at Colgate University where Maxine Greene's *The Dialectic of Freedom* and John Dewey's *The School and Society The Child and the Curriculum* were departmentally negotiated required readings in the American Schools course of the education department. The challenge of the work, then, was to help undergraduate liberal arts students understand these dense and complex texts.

But now, in our social justice–focused master's programs in elementary education at Binghamton, I have continued to develop intentional strategies for the teaching of these works by Dewey and Greene because of what I intimated then that these particular readings were uniquely suited to do: provide compelling spiritualized conceptions of positive social realities, i.e., "wholeness of labor," "dialectic of freedom," that resonate with the (I believe realistically) hopeful beliefs about the potential of children that motivate people to want to become elementary educators. I continue to appreciate how effective study of these texts can encourage in my current students reflection around issues of social construction of both identity and knowledge that does not contradict the deeply spiritual conception of our work that I share with many of them.

In our efforts to pursue social justice through graduate level elementary teacher education at Binghamton University we strategize continually about how to develop the critically self-reflective and caring capacities of our students. I have become increasingly aware of how the conventional course structure in education departments reinforces the dominant culture's tendency to dichotomize these capacities for critical reflection and care, particularly for elementary education students. Social foundations knowledge is still primarily concentrated into separate courses that generally offer only theoretical insight into its transformative potential for the curriculum and the teacher-student relationship. Particularly in larger schools of education the people who teach these courses rarely connect with fieldwork and even enjoy a certain kind of prestige related to their distance from the actual practices of teaching and caring for children in public schools.

The irony is that the knowledge that explains why issues of power and domination in relation to race, class, gender, age, and appearance cannot be treated as add-ons by classroom teachers is often packaged in many universities to look like an add-on, particularly for elementary education students. I am concerned that what amounts to the marginalizing of social foundations knowledge also reinforces a certain kind of anti-intellectualism on the part of elementary education students and teachers who are supported by the broader culture in wrongly assuming both that what is "theoretical" stands in opposition to what is practical and that *what children can handle is the practical.*

Clearly, the specific plans presented here represent a small part of an effort to rethink a graduate program in elementary education both individually and collectively with department colleagues. Inspired by a sometimes discordant choir of teacher-researcher-philosophers, we envision an elementary teacher education program rooted in both careful analysis of texts and community-based social action, where our students develop curriculum collaboratively with teachers, local activists, and children on the basis of *what needs to get done* and *what would improve the quality of life in this community.* Thus, a more visionary context for the work described in this chapter might be a teacher education seminar held in conjunction with a language arts/history fieldwork concentration, in which prospective elementary teachers could challenge themselves as readers and writers while collaborating with classroom teachers and children to develop integrated literacy/history curriculum for their fieldwork site.

To truly integrate the activist focus of our Social Action as Curriculum course with student teaching seminars is a goal to which our own program is moving. Our current activist work will be explored more deeply in Chapter 5 and intimated in Chapters 3 and 4; here I will address primarily that aspect of the curriculum that represents support for that work in the form of moving students to take personally the lessons of John Dewey's *The School and Society The Child and the Curriculum* and Maxine Greene's *The Dialectic of Freedom.*

Why I continue to teach
The School and Society The Child and the Curriculum

I do not discount those who view Dewey's tragic flaw as one he shares with other thinkers and activists of the Progressive Era: a collusion with interests favoring social control, including the "othering" of minorities and identification with American military interests (Feinber, 1972; Katz, 1971). I *do* understand how his work can be used to affirm dominant discourses about race, ethnicity, colonization and immigrant status (Goodenow, 1977; Pittenger, 1997). As well, I have always been sensitive to the potential for inquiry-oriented and constructivist education to become careless of the needs of non-dominant-culture children for instruction in the "codes of the culture of power" (Delpit, 1995). Yet I continue to use this Dewey text with my students because I believe that it voices the very specific role elementary education can play in the pursuit of global social justice through the pursuit of economic equity: it can foster a vision of, even model an enactment of, "the wholeness of labor" (my language), whereby the thinking/directing and doing aspects of labor are not separated and respectively assigned to different people. Related to the above, I see the potential for the use of this "wholeness of labor" paradigm to disrupt all dominant discourses by invalidating the oppressive assumption that some people are thinkers and others are doers.

In speaking to the problems of a division of labor between "cultured people" and "workers" in a text that is a treatise about school curriculum-making, Dewey establishes that the way we are typically expected to learn is antithetical to our humanness in precisely the same way that the way we are expected to work is antithetical to our humanness; further, the fallacy of these parallel expectations is exposed in Dewey's particular wisdom about human beings: most human beings are not drawn to thinking in the abstract but rather want to make and do in a context in which we have the power to think about what, why, and for whom we are making and doing. Then, tying the argument to its compelling implications for the work of elementary teacher education, his text establishes that elementary school is the place to replicate the history of human doing and making; the purpose of elementary education is to retrace the building of human communities and their rationales and to empower children to couple the uncovered knowledge with imagination and discipline in order to address the problems and challenges of the present.

My rationale for the special importance of these insights for my students in this historical era is the following: We are increasingly disconnected from nature, the body, play, and the stuff or viscera of the material world (with the exception of passive experience as consumers). This reality is continually acknowledged by most of my students and colleagues, regardless of our social class, family, or ethnic background, as the universal alienation of this "information age." The Dewey-inspired elementary curriculum unites mind and body, thinking and doing. With its focus on growing things, building, measuring and estimating capacities and distances, exploring the neighborhood's history and the history of the bigger "neighborhoods" that circumscribe ours, it requires immediate engagement with what is. In deciding "what makes sense," predicting "what will happen," and using words to record, invite, and inspire, such a curriculum can become a welcome journey back to a short-lived or once fantasized deep engagement with the world for many of our students and for ourselves. Further, I am finding evidence that some of these enlivened students and teachers move a step further into advocacy or other forms of social activism.

However, appreciating the potential of a particular text and teaching it effectively are two different issues. Although *The School and Society The Child and the Curriculum* is less abstract than much of Dewey's other writing, it is easy to argue that the text is both too dense and disorganized. Dewey's effort to contextualize the University of Chicago labschool curriculum in the endangered social habits of pre-industrial society creates a difficult paradigm shift for readers who have no background in his conception of democracy and the critique of the division of labor that supports that conception. As well, for contemporary readers who see what the marketing of technology has wrought, the style in which Dewey expresses his misplaced faith in technology can seem uncomfortably messianic. Instead of viewing that misplaced faith as a problem to be seriously considered, students can easily become turned off to the entire work.

The challenge, then, is to help students connect their own experience with the social realities Dewey describes. My term for the quality of text that makes such connection likely for my students is *life-text*. It is available in this work by Dewey, but is not as obvious a presence as in *The Dialectic of Freedom*, in which Greene contextualizes her complex inquiry in varied sketches from biographical and imaginative literature so as to present the collectivity of life stories as a kind of embodied theory. I realized early on in my use of the Dewey text that it requires a connecting link in the form of *life-text* that features the aspects of pre-industrial social organization that Dewey so values. Julia Weber Gordon's *My Country School Diary*, introduced in the previous chapter, is such a text. Weber Gordon's book is a four-year-diary of a country school teacher mentored by a student of John Dewey's. Her curriculum includes intervention by the children into the aesthetic, social, and economic realities of their community. (One such intervention, related to the dairy industry, is mentioned in Chapter 1.)

The strategies I have developed for teaching both the Dewey and Greene texts, then, direct the students to their *life-text* content. Although I continue to be attached to what I see as the unique contributions of these texts in particular, I believe that both the orientation to study guides and lesson-planning and the understanding of the special value of *life-text* described in this chapter is transferable to work with other texts.

Use of study guides

My practice is to offer study guides as very specific supports for my students' independent reading of text. My purpose is to direct the author's words to the (integrated) mind-body that Dewey equated with human mental, physical, and spiritual health, even when the study guide is for a text other than Dewey's! In other words, I want the text to speak to what is most healthy and hopeful in my students, to the place in them that already sees the division of labor as antithetical to their humanness. The goal is to elicit response in the form of thinking that has implications for action in their classrooms and in the world.

I articulate to my students that I hope they will adapt such an orientation to study guides for the younger learners in their own future classrooms. I view these guides as part of my commitment to social reconstructionist teaching, whereby my students and I collaborate under my leadership to understand and further develop the resources (including their own) that I hope will help us pursue a more socially just future for schools and the communities that circumscribe them.

These study guides model that we get knowledge from a wide variety of sources by drawing from a range of concepts formally explored in courses to very personal contributions of students in class that I request their permission to include. They often refer to other texts, to realities of our lives outside of school, to the students' current classroom internships, and to personal history and memories. They include alternative (to dictionary definition) approaches to defining key words and concepts, and specific references to my own and even their own "aha!" moments of understanding related to my current collaboration with them to understand the text.

I ask questions that offer students a handle with which to grab an idea they might have experienced as abstract, or I offer a clue to personal connection with a different historical era. My goal is always the same: to move them toward ownership of knowledge that I believe will help them develop into better teachers and social justice–focused activists.

With regard to modeling parallel practices, it is important to note that the typical culture of public schools will rapidly draw new teachers into a more mechanistic approach to asking questions about text; the motivation for such questioning is more often than not to test to see if children have done the reading. It is critical that we work to draw our students into an alternative culture of literacy, where people read in order to make sense of their own lives. Such sense-making then raises possibilities for new forms of healing, beauty, and activism in both their own lives and in the life of their communities. I make the assumption that only teacher education students who have internalized such a rich conception of literacy will effectively promote it with children.

I specifically encourage my students to meet outside of class in informal study groups in order to collectively tackle the relevant questions after they have read the assigned portion of the text. But I strongly advise that they study the questions before they begin to read the text and that while reading they make liberal notations, including and especially page numbers correlated to key words and inspiring passages. I suggest that they make these notations in their own books, on Post-it notes, or in a separate reading journal. In class when we review the study guides, I continually insist on text-based responses, even as I simultaneously pull for dialectical connections with their own life experience, with the responses of classmates, and with other texts.

I have found the following study guide particularly useful to my students after they have experienced the pinchpot lesson featured in Chapter 1.

Study guide for John Dewey's The School and Society The Child and the Curriculum

1) Dewey's work is often trivialized through use of the catch-phrase learning by doing. Yet *doing* certainly has an important place in his curriculum, particularly with primary and elementary age children. How exactly does *doing* fit into his model? What is the relationship between doing, thinking and pre-industrial family/community life as portrayed by Dewey? Read aloud the long passages of his description of the child's place in pre-industrial family/community life. Do you experience any identification with some aspect(s) of your own childhood, or any sense of loss or of having missed out when you read Dewey's (granted, possibly a bit romanticized) portrayal of this life?

2) Your introduction tells you that "Dewey's outlook was a contested point of view." Why does behaviorism stand in direct opposition to Dewey's thinking about how people learn and grow? Can you hypothesize why behaviorism was so popular in the historical period in which Dewey wrote this book? Where/When have you seen behaviorism as a guiding philosophy operative in the classroom/school in which you are interning?

3) Understand that Dewey sees the industrial revolution as the change that "overshadows and even controls all others" and makes necessary his project of "modernizing" education. How does Dewey feel about the death of pre-industrial family/community life? At the same time, do you see his general

enthusiasm about the growth of technology? Read aloud the passages that capture this enthusiasm. Can you tell how he feels about the capitalist economic system under whose auspices these rapid changes are taking place?

4) Really study Dewey's argument against the division of labor (into thinking/managing work and doing work). With regard to data that supports Dewey's argument: Recall our brainstorming session during the first class when students addressed the question, "What childhood experiences made you feel the most intelligent and useful?" Rob responded with a description of his extended family's yearly gathering at his grandparents' farm to "do the haying." S. spoke of collaborating with her retarded sister to compile and caption a family photo album specifically featuring the relationship between the two sisters. Dewey makes what he calls occupations the basis of his primary/elementary level curriculum. Justify the use of "occupations" as the starting point of the curriculum given Dewey's critique of the division of labor and his assertion in this part of the text about what it is that most people want to use their thinking for. Do you identify with his conception of what people want to use their thinking for?

5) How does Dewey's conception of the division of labor connect with his insistence that occupations-based education is "permeated throughout with the spirit of art, history, and science"? What is Dewey's notion of an "intellectual"? How is it that he believes that very few of us are intellectuals but that all of us would appreciate an education "permeated throughout with the spirit of art, history, and science"?

6) Study Dewey's use of the word/concept "discipline." How does it contrast and/or conform to your own understanding of that word through your own schooling? How does it contrast and/or conform to the use of that word in the school in which you are interning? Recall our consideration of behaviorism. Can you see how one's perspective on how people learn and grow might affect their conception of discipline?

7)   Study Dewey's use of the word/concept "imagination." Construct an inquiry/critique of the meanings of this word using as inspiration my construction of #6 above. See if in your group at least one of you can recall a teacher presenting to you an "opportunity to use your imagination" in the way Dewey ridicules, and conversely, in the way Dewey appreciates.

8)   What are Dewey's objections to "manual training" and/or vocational education and how does his critique of the division of labor inform his objections?

9)   What is the "medieval conception of learning" that Dewey identifies with "present education"? In what ways is this "medieval conception of learning" consonant with the division of labor?

10)   Where do books fit into the Dewey curriculum? How does the floor plan of Dewey's school reflect a respect for the study of literature and history, particularly in the upper school? Why are subjects okay then, in the upper school, according to Dewey?

11)   What challenges to Dewey's thinking and Julia Weber Gordon's practices do you see in multiculturalism? Related, most of you have studied Erica Burman's critique of child-centeredness (1994) in Monica's Child Growth course. How does that critique apply to Dewey?

12)   Recall the concerns expressed in class about separation of church and state issues when I (positively) characterized as "soulwork" Vivian Paley's description of her own teaching in *The Boy Who Would Be a Helicopter*. In my own scholarly writing I argue that spirituality informs Dewey's thinking. Do you see any indication of what you would call spiritual concerns in this book? In Julia Weber Gordon's classroom? Does any aspect of Julia's curriculum raise separation of church and state concerns for you?

13)   In his own life Dewey advocated for socialism, which has as its goal the achievement of a workers' democracy. Is Julia Weber Gordon's classroom a learner democracy? How and how not? Related, as teachers and future teachers, how do we

separate the legitimate leadership roles of adults in relation to children from oppression of children by adults? How does our own potential collusion with the bureaucracies of schooling complicate the above issues? Where/How do these same issues play out in my (B. R.'s) teaching of this course?

My tentative discoveries

I have found the last segment of the last study guide question critically important in countering both the feeling and actuality of the teacher-directed nature of the assignment of an intellectually orienting study guide like this one. Students who will be teachers need to confront the reality of their power to help shape the thinking of their students. What more effective way to confront this power than to examine the somewhat analogous nature of the relationship between the instructor and the students' own educational processes, while at the same time making them aware of the instructor's awareness of the contradictions in the pedagogical approaches she has chosen?

Another practice I have found very useful in countering the teacher-directed focus of the review of study guide responses is an in-class round-robin read-aloud of "personally inspiring passages" from our text. In fact, I developed the question about personal feelings of identification or loss in #1 above in response to so many students wanting to read aloud Dewey's descriptions of pre-industrial rural family/community life. When the round-robin immediately precedes review of the study guide responses, a particularly lovely dynamic has been created: students read as poetry many of the same passages from the text we will later review as data collected in response to the study guide questions. With regard to my own intention to continually suggest the parallel practices of their own work with children, I always hope that this experience elicits for future elementary teachers the potential poetry in living one's life as a reader/researcher continually open to new inspiration.

I note here again that our small elementary education master's program at SUNY Binghamton is ideologically committed, in that we have designed and publicly describe our orientation as "social justice–focused." We, therefore, encounter some of the resistance and social contradictions playing out in class typically reported in scholarly journals by feminist, multiculturalist, and social class–aware professors like ourselves. My experience has been that the use of study guides in conjunction with dense texts like Dewey's creates a culture of intellectual seriousness in which the goal of understanding text at a deep level can override identity and power conflicts. The professor and her own ideological commitments (and therefore, biases), although built into the work, are removed from center stage while students grapple with ideas in their own community of support and then report back to the larger group, typically with some commitment to collectively negotiated understandings.

More than once an individual student has interrupted her/his presentation of a response to a study guide question to ask a fellow study group member for permission to include an interpretation or comment viewed as personal that was shared in their small group. Students have reported that the study guide helps them collect data from the text and from their lives in support of political perspectives they might have conceived of as both "radical" and foreign to their own sometimes not-consciously-interpreted experience.

In a recent set of course evaluations students specifically appreciated the study guides and complained about our sometimes erratic attention to them in class; two students wrote that the use of them made it more likely that they, as shy people, would contribute more actively in class discussion; a few others commented that the professor's ideas "could dominate" when the discussion was not structured by the study guides around student response; a number of students noted that the study guides raised the intellectual level of both their independent reading and our conversations in class.

Inspired by these comments and my own assessment of the usefulness of these guides, I have recently planned a specific assignment for the students in my next curriculum class: to develop a study guide for a selected piece of literature they want to introduce to the children in the classroom of their half-day internships, modeling their work on *our* study guides. I am also making a commitment to more consistent use of student reporting based on their work in response to the study guides. I believe that my resistance to more consistent review of their responses has been my own desire to mask the power I hold and have used to direct their reading/learning with such fierce intentionality.

Rationale for teaching *The Dialectic of Freedom*

Despite initial student resistance to its density and complexity, *The Dialectic of Freedom* (Greene, 1988) is a classic text that has successfully introduced social foundations knowledge to a number of my elementary education graduate students. I believe that the book is important for elementary teachers because it contextualizes an inquiry about what schools could/should do in an interpretive framework that is in equal measure morally compelling and intellectually challenging. It actively makes sense of over a hundred years of American social history by tracing the dialectical process whereby individuals and groups were guided in their intellectual and activist responses to historical developments by the range of possibilities created by the thinkers and *actors* who preceded them.

I have found that many of our students have not previously assimilated an interpretive framework that has made historical knowledge either accessible or useful to them. In Greene's text they are exposed to such an interpretive framework that is particularly compelling in that it transfers to the work they must do in their classrooms! Elementary teachers collaborating with children to shape new knowledge in social reconstructionist classrooms will need to strategize continually about how and where to introduce to the children necessary background information as well as a spiritual/moral/political framework that addresses *what this work is for*. Essentially, they need to see themselves as the motor behind a dialectical process similar to the one Maxine Greene models.

This text accomplishes something else that I see as particularly effective for elementary educators. As previously stated, Greene contextualizes her complex inquiry in varied sketches from biographical and imaginative literature so as to present the collectivity of life stories as a kind of embodied theory. These passages that I call *life-text* demystify social theory by illustrating how it is spun from observation of the complex realities of people's lives, including their thinking, limitations and actions. Greene also provides the conceptual framework for using biographies and contemporary multicultural fiction, other sources for *life-texts*, in our work in the university classroom and in our students' work as teachers. (See Chapter 5.) I have come to believe that *life-text* has a special place in the education of elementary teachers, many of whom have a positive view of children as natural storytellers as well as an appreciation of the storytelling art involved in good teaching.

We know from the constructivist/social constructionist paradigms that heavily influence our work that the texts we use must provide an entry point for our students. The entry point that I've been able to make accessible for my students is Greene's introduction, early on, of the concept of "situatedness" borrowed from the philosopher Charles Taylor. The idea of all of our life stories/experience being *situated* by birth, ethnicity, class background, and geography provides a non-threatening bridge to the exploration of both the social construction of each of us as individuals and of the course participants as a unit, possibly representative of teachers in general. At the same time, the complex links between *situatedness* and patterns of thinking are demystified through Greene's continual attention to the dialectical and historical evolution of the *thinkability* of specific ideas. ("How can I make certain important ideas *thinkable* in my classroom?" is a particularly useful question for elementary teachers.)

Yet there is never the sense that the dialectic proceeds mechanically; rather, the lyricism of the text speaks to the spirituality that compels acting on *thinkable* ideas. Because Greene refuses to reduce her argument to oppression theory, she carries along the students who are better *situated* to identify with specific actors on the basis of a commitment to *overcome obstacles* (Greene's phrase) in a more general spiritual sense. Then this identification, once in place, can lead students to a deeper understanding of how a person's social construction helps to determine what presents itself as an *obstacle* to be *overcome*. At the same time, the whole notion of a *dialectic of freedom* introduces an educative framework for understanding the importance of collective, as well as individual action.

However, the related concepts of social construction of identity/ knowledge/reality introduced through the consideration of *situatedness* were difficult for many of my students; for some of them understanding the importance of collective action was also abstract. I recognized that students needed to use these concepts to examine real choices made by real people in order to understand them. Yet the many moments of choice in the many lives set in dialectical relation to one another in Greene's text were sometimes experienced as overwhelming, particularly by readers with weaker backgrounds in literature and history.

Since first being introduced to this text I have strategized about how to effectively work with my students on *The Dialectic of Freedom* in the context of a gradual realization that courses with heavy social foundations content require a careful balance between the promotion of student-centered discussion and strong teacher leadership. Unless students can actively construct their understandings in the public context of the university classroom, both passivity and the unfortunate tendency to decontextualize personal values from issues of power and domination are reinforced. Yet I have never seen the typical model of laissez-faire discussion loosely based on the assigned readings significantly move students to seriously reconsider their assumptions about their own privilege, or about power, morality, and the status of democracy in the United States.

I have found that the presentation in class of certain kinds of contemporary articles from the popular media has made it possible to isolate and examine moments of choice in the lives of particular actors. Use of these short readings in group-work has empowered students to take risks in identifying elements of social construction "situatedness" they could uncover in the *life-text* with which they were presented.

The following is the first of two lesson plans I have developed and used with my students. This one requires the accompanying Ku Klux Klan Widow article which immediately follows the assignment:

Assignment based on the Dialectic of Freedom

Read and reread the attached article that originally appeared in the *New York Times* on September 4, 1993. Working in small groups identify every aspect of Henry Alexander's "situatedness" that would have made the horrendous crime he committed *conceivable*.

I emphasized the word "conceivable" because we are not suggesting here that Henry Alexander's crime is in any way *excusable*, just that many aspects of his situatedness made it *thinkable*. This part of the assignment, therefore, takes place outside of the realm of an essentialist conception of morality and outside of the realm of judgments about deserved punishment.

In addition to factors in Henry Alexander's personal life, consider the social climate of this part of the South at that time in history with regard to issues of race. (Be sure to include the way government officials at many levels responded to the crime and the experience of Willie Edward's widow after the crime.) These factors were aspects of the environment in which Henry Alexander was situated.

Now remember our discussion about *dialectical thinking being a kind of directional thinking.* Consider any *movement in the direction of what Greene would identify as freedom* on the part of any of the players in this story. Explain the individual obstacles moved against (by any player) in each behavior that directed itself toward freedom.

This process of moving against obstacles (in both the broadest and the most concrete specific sense) represents one type of operation of *the dialectic of freedom,* according to Greene.

Now propose any action that might be generated by any of the players in the Ku Klux Klan Widow article in the future (outside of the time frame of the newspaper story) which would keep *the dialectic of freedom* going or moving.

Widow Inherits a Confession To a 36-Year-Old Hate Crime
By Adam Nossiter
Special to The New York Times.
Copyright @ 1993 by the New York Times Co. Reprinted by Permission.

MONTGOMERY, Ala. —It was well after midnight one chilly winter more than 36 years ago. Four white men and one black man stood on the Tyler Goodwin Bridge, in a deserted area near here. Fifty feet below, the Alabama River flowed briskly.

The white men were Ku Klux Klansmen. They had driven the black man through the dark countryside, terrorizing him. He had said something offensive to a white woman, they said, and he was going to pay. Now, on the bridge, one Klansman pointed his gun at the young man and said, "Hit the water."

Screaming, the black man leaped to his death. Back in town, the four white men joked that he had jumped in for a swim. Three months later, in April 1957, two fishermen found the decomposed body of Willie Edwards Jr. 10 miles west of Montgomery.

None of the men on the bridge that night were ever punished: an aggressive Alabama attorney general, Bill Baxley, stumbled onto the case in 1976, but a judge threw out charges twice. Now the widow of one of the men who was accused, but never tried, 17 years ago says her husband owned up to the crime in the months before his death last year.

The widow, Diane Alexander, is reaching out to the family of the man who died in the river long ago, trying to write the last chapter in the story of her husband, Henry Alexander, a Klansman. His remorse and her shame for his role in a murderous history illuminate a larger transformation in Alabama's tortured race relations.

Mrs. Alexander has written a sorrowful letter of apology to Mr. Edwards's widow, Sarah Jean Salter, who lives in Buffalo now. "I hope maybe one day I can meet you to tell you face to face how sorry I am," the letter said. "May God bless you and your family and I pray that this letter helps you somehow."

And on Sept. 4, in Montgomery, she will meet with the Edwards's grown daughter, Melinda O'Neill, who was 3 when her father was killed. Mrs. Alexander wants to express her shame in person.

Confession: A Klan member reveals a secret. As a young man, Henry Alexander was one of the leading foot soldiers in the Montgomery Klan. But before he died of lung cancer last December at 63, he made a confession, Diane Alexander says.

Two days after Thanksgiving last year, Henry Alexander walked into Diane's beauty shop. They were alone. They both knew the end was coming. He sat down in her chair.

She describes what happened next as a turning point in her life:

"Mama, I need to talk to you," her husband said. Diane Alexander, a heavy-set, good-natured woman, thought he was going to launch into another of their interminable family spats.

"I don't even know what God has planned for me," Henry continued. "I don't even know how to pray for myself."

Diane Alexander was mystified.

"I got things bothering me," her husband said.

"What things are bothering you?" she asked.

"Well, Willie Edwards."

He told his wife that Willie Edwards would not have died if he had not falsely identified Mr. Edwards as the one who had offended the white woman. "I'm the one that told 'em," Mr. Alexander said. On the bridge that night, he said, he and the other Klansmen gave Mr. Edwards a choice: run or jump. "I didn't think he would jump," he said. "If he'd a run, they would never have shot him."

Diane Alexander was silent. Then her shock turned to anger. She felt sick, she says now, disgusted. She was Henry's third wife, and she had been loyal to him. All at once she realized that her years of believing his innocence in the Edwards killing had been pointless.

"Henry left me with absolutely nothing, except his guilt of what he done to Willie Edwards," Diane Alexander said bitterly. "Henry lived a lie all his life, and he made me live it, too."

She says she wanted to tell this story. But Henry's family was deaf to it. His son by an earlier marriage, Steve, like other family members interviewed, says he does not believe his father was involved in the death of Willie Edwards or had ever said so.

But others, outside the family, believe Diane Alexander is telling the truth, including the family minister, the Rev. Lenny Bolton, and a black man Henry Alexander put in charge of the work crew of his pipe-fitting business, Dorsey Thompson. Jack Shows, a bluff Montgomery policeman who dogged Mr. Alexander for much of his life, was not surprised to hear the story Diane Alexander is telling. And Sarah Jean Salter, the widow of Willie Edwards, stunned by Diane Alexander's letter, is convinced of the woman's sincerity.

Mrs. Alexander's life is disordered. She lives here in a small cottage, neat outside but inside a chaos of tattered furniture, dirty dishes, half-cooked food on the stove and scattered toys of her three grandchildren, of whom she has custody.

In a back room, detritus from Henry Alexander's life spills from a table: a loose pile of his clippings, his White Citizens' Council membership card, the pattern for his Klan hood used by a local seamstress, a braided leather whip he carried in Klan marches. Henry Alexander did not want his children to see these mementos. But he preserved them, testimony to the ambivalent pride he took in his past.

"He wanted to be important," Mrs. Alexander said. "He wanted to be a somebody. Well, what Henry done to be important, Henry lived to regret it."

The killing: 'Begging for his life.' Henry Alexander was born in Montgomery on May 8, 1929. His father was an itinerant plumbing subcontractor, his mother the granddaughter of a Reconstruction-era Ku Klux Klansman. She died when Henry was 7. His father, C. A. Alexander, who was known as a strident racist, was frequently absent. Young Henry was put into a boarding house at the age of 12 and made to go to work when he was in junior high school. "It was a brutal, hard life," Steve Alexander said.

The most violent phase of the white reaction to the civil rights movement here, in 1956 and 1957, coincided with Henry Alexander's young manhood. The boycott of Montgomery's bus lines, organized by blacks to protest segregated seating, was ending, and Henry was entering the underground war against integration. Some of his life in the Klan can be seen in court documents, old clippings and interviews.

There were petty acts of harassment in those months: Mr. Alexander helped jump a black man, he flipped lighted cigarettes into the vehicles of blacks, cruised around town throwing rocks at integrated buses, fired a .38-caliber pistol into the side of one bus, hitting a pregnant black woman in the legs.

In the early hours of Jan. 10, 1957, bombs went off all over Montgomery. Mr. Alexander was later charged with setting one off, an explosion that destroyed the front of the house of the Rev. Ralph David Abernathy, the civil rights leader. "He laughed about it," Diane Alexander said of her husband. "He thought it was funny." Those charges against him were dropped.

One evening about 10 days later, a group of men was sitting around the Little Kitchen restaurant, a Klan hangout, discussing what they considered a noxious affront: a black truck driver for the Winn-Dixie supermarket chain, on the run between Montgomery and Sylacauga, a small town about 40 miles northeast of here, was said to have made an offensive remark to a white woman.

Nineteen years later, Mr. Baxley, the attorney general who had been looking into several unsolved civil rights cases, was told about the Edwards killing. Then he found one of the Klansmen, Raymond Britt, who told investigators for the attorney general what had happened next.

On Jan. 23, 1957, Mr. Britt got a telephone call: rendezvous at Henry Alexander's house. Carrying pistols and other guns, four Klansmen piled into a car. With Henry Alexander at the wheel, the men drove up and down the highway. Around 11:30 P.M, they spotted a truck parked near a grocery store. Driving past it again, they read the logo: Winn-Dixie.

Inside the truck was Willie Edwards Jr. He had stopped at the store to get a soft drink on his way home. It had been his first trip to Sylacauga. This was not his normal route; he had been called in to substitute for a sick driver. Supporting his pregnant wife, two children and two sisters, Mr. Edwards kept a wary distance from the civil rights ferment in his hometown. Two months on the job, he had quickly agreed to fill in when his new bosses at Winn-Dixie called on him that afternoon.

Mr. Edwards turned his dome light on to read his logbook. The Klansmen had a clear view inside the cab. Henry Alexander turned his car around and pulled up in front of the Winn-Dixie truck. It was about 10 minutes before midnight.

Mr. Britt and another Klansman got out. They walked over to the truck. At gunpoint, Willie Edwards was ordered into the car.

His truck, with its lights on, remained there by the store, where it was found the next day.

The Klansmen drove off. They started in at once, shoving and slapping. Who was he? they demanded. What was his name? What had he said to the white woman? Mr. Edwards "was very frightened and pleaded with us not to harm him," Mr. Britt remembered. Over and over, Mr. Edwards denied having said anything to any white woman. Pointing his gun at Mr. Edwards, one Klansman threatened to castrate him for harassing the white woman.

The men drove to the Tyler Goodwin bridge. Mr. Edwards was "sobbing and begging for his life," Mr. Britt told the investigators. Diane Alexander said it had been Henry who insisted to the others that they had found the right man.

The police quickly closed their books on the disappearance of the Winn-Dixie driver. Willie Edwards's 23-year-old wife, Sarah Jean, frantic with grief and anxiety, said she "just about went batty with it." Alone with three small children to raise, she had very little money. No one had information for her, no lawyer would look into it and her husband's employers offered neither help nor comfort. She saw a psychiatrist. "It was just so strange and so terrible and so upsetting," she remembered. "I couldn't understand it." She left Montgomery with her children in 1961 and never moved back.

Prosecution: Murder charges and a failed case. Diane Alexander remembers her first glimpse of her husband. It was one night around 1961, and she was a teen-ager on a date. Out of the door of a seedy downtown cafe came a wiry, tough-looking fellow and a stoutish woman. They were fighting furiously, cussing each other and going at it, literally fist and nail, right out in the street. The man's face was all scratched up. This was Henry Alexander, Diane learned.

Ten years later she was working as a waitress, at a Shoney's here, when Henry Alexander noticed her. He pursued her, and she soon moved in. He was a moderately successful contractor who had inherited his father's business. He yearned to be respectable, influential. In later years, one of his most prized possessions was a photograph of himself between Montgomery's Mayor and police chief, taken at a civic function.

"I want you to get our stuff together," he told her one day in February

1976. "As soon as I pay the boys, me and you are gonna go to Florida. Don't tell anybody we're going. Let's just go."

She didn't know what was going on, but she didn't ask too many questions. Back at the house, she spotted the state troopers moving from the yard into the office. She remembers the exchange:

"Are you Henry Alexander?"

"What's going on?"

"We have a warrant for your arrest."

Bill Baxley, the attorney general troubled by his state's murderous past, was uncovering old secrets. He was scanning every Southern hate group he could think of, and he was talking to ex-Klansmen. One of them told the young attorney general, "I got out of the Klan when they killed the Winn-Dixie clerk." This was something Mr. Baxley knew nothing about. That's when he persuaded Raymond Britt to confess, gave him immunity and filed first-degree murder charges against three men: Henry Alexander, Jimmy York and Sonny Kyle Livingston.

For Willie Edwards's family, Mr. Baxley's efforts were both an extraordinary relief and deeply painful. His daughter Melinda, then 23, quit her job in Buffalo and moved back to Montgomery to follow the case in court. "It was sort of difficult for everybody," she remembered.

Problems began to develop for the prosecutors. For one thing, the body of Willie Edwards was so badly decomposed that it had been impossible to determine a cause of death.

This bothered the judge, who quashed the indictment twice, insisting that a cause of death had to be specified. "Merely forcing a person to jump from a bridge does not naturally and probably lead to the death of such a person," Judge Frank Embry ruled. Mr. Baxley thought the judge was wrong. But then Mr. Britt decided that Mr. Livingston hadn't been there after all, and that man passed a lie-detector test.

Mr. Baxley and his team were discouraged. Then an unexpected development helped finish off the dying case. Agents from the Federal Bureau of Investigation came to the attorney general "requesting and begging" that he leave Henry Alexander alone. Mr Alexander had been their best informant in the Klan. Mr. Baxley was stunned. But the agents' pleading helped him decide that proceeding was pointless. A former F.B.I. agent in Montgomery, Clifford Rowe, refuses to say whether Henry Alexander was involved with the Bureau.

Remorse: No escaping a conscience. Even before the talk with his wife at her beauty shop that day last year, there were hints that Henry Alexander was not hewing as fast to his old positions.

"I've done some pretty bad things," he said once to a Bible study group at his house. His minister, the Rev. Lenny Bolton, was listening. Henry seemed to be edging up to contrition. But then he backed away. "Nothing real bad," he continued. "Me and the boys threw some bombs at some niggers."

Not long after, doctors diagnosed the cancer that made him weak and was soon to kill him. In the final weeks, Mrs. Alexander says, she remembers he was often unable to sleep and would get up and stumble into the yard. "My life hasn't meant nothing," he told her early one morning.

She tried to comfort him. But his revelations had thrown her life into turmoil. "How have you lived with this?" Diane asked him. Henry replied that there hadn't been a day that it hadn't bothered him.

In the final week, his torment seemed to increase. He "just worried and worried," Diane said, and she "constantly had to touch him and say, 'Henry, everything is going to be all right.'" He had himself baptized. It didn't calm him. Four days before he died, he sat out in the front yard and cried.

"I had no business hating the blacks," he mumbled. "They've never done anything to me." Then, trying to cheer himself, Henry Alexander chuckled and said, "That man, he'll probably open the door for me."

Deconstruction in class

In my experience with this assignment, a consistent pattern has been the resistance of a few students to move beyond a conception of Henry Alexander as inherently evil and able to confess his monstrous crime only because of his fear of retribution in death. The discussion this enforces about what is essential to a human being versus what is nurtured and/or created by culture is a critical one for prospective and practicing elementary teachers. Many contradictions emerge about faith in the potential of education and experience to shape people's intelligence versus belief in essential realities, truths, and limitations. But the assignment is specifically structured to circumvent the defensiveness that often surfaces when *social construction* is introduced. The idea is to offer students the opportunity to actively deconstruct the *construction* of a person from whom they feel (and wish to remain) distanced, even completely dissociated. Further, because the subject/object of this deconstruction exercise is a Ku Klux Klansman, students do not initially need to confront the racism they have necessarily internalized no matter how well intentioned in order to feel completely justified in distancing themselves morally from him. Yet this process of moral distancing is immediately called into question by the students themselves when they begin to consider the data about this confessed racist and murderer's social construction, which they must do in order to participate in their small groups.

A young man of color at Colgate who had previously identified himself as a Christian and who had rarely spoken out in whole-group discussions suggested that the white people in the class would need to consider the possibility that all white people were evil if they were willing to dismiss Henry Alexander as an anomaly. He charged that white students had no conception of how bad and prevalent racism was, and underestimated the extent to which evil was held in check by laws and by fear. More recently a white working-class elementary education student made a similar argument, and also pointed out that collective action was about changing laws to keep "bad ideas" in check.

In my most recent experience with this assignment when the groups reported back to the class the results of their work on the last question, two groups offered variations on the idea that Diane Alexander, the Ku Klux Klan widow in the article, could start an organization for other Klan wives and widows. One of the groups further suggested that eventually the members of such a group might find the safety in numbers to confront the painful secrets they held in common. Students saw the possibility of collective action in the form of speakouts against Klan activity emerging from a Klan wives organization. Another group (in class) proposed that these women might want to share their life stories with teenage women in local schools. A practicing elementary teacher suggested that children might interview Diane Alexander about how her own attitudes about people of color were shaped and changed.

Encouraged to supply the class with comparable short readings for our continuing study of *The Dialectic of Freedom* one student brought in a *Time* magazine article (January 8, 1996) about the textile manufacturer Carl Fuerstein, who did not allow any employees to lose pay or their jobs when his Massachusetts Polartec factory was destroyed by fire the previous winter. A key passage in the article quotes Fuerstein vehemently denying the sainthood ascribed him by one resident of his town. He goes on to assert that the decline in corporate ethics in recent years has created a climate in which his own reasonable behavior looks saintly.

This powerful example of "social construction of morality" elicited audible "Now I understand[s]!" and generated comparable examples from the class. Two students were able to link this example with their own experience working in schools where humiliation of children was tolerated, as opposed to schools where it clearly was not. One student realized that her former building's climate made certain kinds of humiliation of children appear normal and acceptable practice. A young man, E., whose father had been laid off after twenty years as a middle manager at IBM, pointed out that his father's guilt about being unemployed was socially constructed. I asked teachers to think about their attitudes, whether they expressed them directly or not, toward employed and unemployed parents of children in their classes in light of E.'s comment. Could teachers identify the ways in which they were both victims and perpetrators of these often subtle forces of social control?

A mother in the class realized aloud that she felt guilty yelling at her own children in front of some people but not in front of others. Her question to us: What does it mean when we behave better in front of some people than others?

This discussion provided the appropriate groundwork for me to formally introduce the concept of "dominant culture" and to begin to examine how the dominant culture imposes on schools the standards for whom and what is worthy versus unworthy, who deserves power, and what kinds of children are likely to learn about the specific contributions to our society of groups with which they identify. I have learned to balance such mini-lecture/discussions, which can inspire a silencing level of guilt on the part of white middle-class students, with a consideration of Greene's conception of a possible "public good" based on a notion of dignity available to everyone.

I asked students to consider in small groups and report back to the whole group, if they chose to, a personal example of taking a social risk inspired by a concern for the public good or a need to overcome obstacles or maintain dignity. Students have reported speaking out while in the company of friends in disapproval of racist jokes, put-downs of fat people, and ridicule of nonconforming peers. Two students who were teachers in the same school reported subtly affecting the culture of their teachers' room by politely but firmly refusing to listen to stereotypical judgments about poor families. One student spoke of acting against harassment of gay and lesbian students in his high school as a high school student, once through the school newspaper and once by addressing a PTA meeting. Another reported participating in a vigil in honor of Native Americans on Columbus Day, moved, he reported, by a confrontation with a girlfriend from South America.

These last two comments allowed me to introduce the idea that consideration of both homosexuality and colonization were absent from *The Dialectic of Freedom*. A student who identified himself as a Christian asked what he was supposed do about his religious conviction that homosexuality was wrong. A fascinating and heated discussion followed in which a number of students insisted that certain attitudes were inconsistent with teaching in public schools. One student left the classroom briefly when the young man who had spoken of his girlfriend from South America compared racism to intolerance of homosexuality.

A young white woman, shifting the discussion to the more academic considerations I had originally hoped to address, suggested with a smile that she felt we would not reach agreement on "these political issues." After examining the publication date of the text, she proposed that the book was printed too early for these issues to be included. "They weren't viewed as quite so critical for teachers yet in 1988." A review of the text's concept of how ideas become "thinkable" ensued. Students were generally moved by my interpretation that the very inclusion in our current class discussion of the reports (by the two students) about both advocating for gays and lesbians and attending the Columbus Day vigil could affect what was included in a future text like *The Dialectic of Freedom*, written by one of us or by others exposed to similar discussion of different people's life experience. Maxine Greene, I pointed out, had spoken directly about both issues when she had addressed our BU School of Education and Human Development at a special lecture earlier that term. I asked the students to consider how motivating it could be for new immigrant children (of whom there are many in the local schools) to have their stories welcomed in classrooms where teachers understood and articulated that knowledge was under active construction, not only for this classroom community, but also for future classes and texts.

But I also offered the interpretation that conflict was difficult to sustain in the classroom and that it had been more comfortable for students to address my question from an academic perspective than to experience deeply felt differences of perspective about issues of race and sexual preference. Because I was very comfortable with the student who had smiled and attempted to address my more limited initial intentions, I was able to comment that I had observed over time that many young women drawn to elementary teaching had been, like myself, "good girls" who kept the peace in our families of origin.

My experience has been that class sessions like this one have left many students newly able to hear marginalized voices and marginalized conceptions of history in other books, films, and autobiographical presentations. They also seem to confirm the reality that disagreement, facing but also tolerating contradictions, and strong feelings are necessary content in classes that deal critically with issues of race, class, and gender.

Most promising to me from a pedagogical perspective is that in my last two experiences teaching this text the following question emerged and then proceeded to organize the rest of the course: What would it mean for me/us/you (individually and/or collectively) to seize the *dialectic of freedom* in the classrooms in which we are currently teaching or interning? The public legitimizing of this question has led to continual restatement of the idea that we probably have more power than we think we have to influence the environments in which people of all ages are relating to young people.

A few class participants took seriously this realization in relation to fellow students. Duplicated readings about the importance of teachers explicitly valuing in their classrooms the languages and dialects children speak at home (while simultaneously providing instruction in dominant culture English) were supplied and assigned by a student who was a recent Russian immigrant. A practicing elementary teacher distributed an article about social action projects that were part of one district's elementary curriculum. Another reviewed a video by an Ithaca filmmaker who had captured the uniquely playful and mutually protective community spirit of the very poor white residents of a well-known old rural road in the area. This already practicing teacher also described how the film had influenced her to do a much appreciated home visit to the family of a young student of hers who lived on this road. Most inspiring was her reported subsequent reevaluation of the strengths of her poor rural students.

My experience has been that students who can be drawn into *The Dialectic of Freedom* often have these "aha" moments of recognizing what it means to self-reflect in the context of an increasingly sophisticated understanding of issues of power, authority, and morality related to race, class, and gender. It appears that getting through the text becomes intertwined with taking it personally. I believe that this happens because the text sets up a spiritual challenge in the context of a reading experience that is very demanding intellectually. The spiritual challenge, the challenge to act on behalf of a group of people, resonates with those who are drawn to teaching out of the consciously well-intentioned desire to make things better for children. Therefore, students can begin to engage positively while simultaneously experiencing the limitations of their own knowledge base, and by extension, the limited nature of their initial conception of what it means to be a teacher. Pulled to identify with many *actors* who are presented as having seized the *dialectic of freedom* readers also see that this engagement with the dialectic is part of the process of growth of these actors.

Yet the very notion of an essential or unproblematic conception of *growth* is interrogated, with students newly able to identify social construction at work in the growth of the individual actor(s) and often by extension, themselves. Fortunately, the construction of the text essentially mirrors the dialectical operation of the struggle in the direction of freedom that the text's *actors* model. Because the teaching challenge for me has been the process of drawing students into the text by literally piercing what some of them perceive as its impenetrability, use of this mirroring reality has been particularly productive. I developed the following (second) lesson plan in response to these issues.

Study guide (exercise) for chapters 2 and 3 or 2 and 4 of the **Dialectic of Freedom**

As we discussed in our last class, *The Dialectic of Freedom* is a text whose message is mirrored in its structure. What is perhaps even more significant is that in order to read the text successfully you need to build dialectically on your own knowledge base.

You have now seen that the above conception of the text is echoed by Bob Gowin in the foreword, page x. "Perhaps for educators, the dialectic between received authority of external knowledge is in tension with the constructivist view that human knowledge is a human construction. The notion of knowledge given antecedently and independently of knowers, Maxine [Greene] rejects. In her dialectic, the knower and the known are co-present, each modifying and shaping the other."

This "assignment" will cause you to immerse yourself in the (constructivist) dialectical construction of both the text and its (the text's) relationship to you and what you know. Read the text at least through Chapter 3 before you begin this exercise.

1) Choose any one of Greene's textual references that you already have knowledge about and explain (to yourself or a friend) how what you already know and thought made it possible to understand the place of this particular reference in the line of thinking she is building. Trace how your previous knowledge enabled you to connect this reference with her use of a previous

reference or following reference. In what context did you acquire the knowledge that helped you? Was a line of thinking different from, similar to, or totally unrelated to Greene's being built at that time? Or did you acquire this knowledge in a decontextualized manner, not having associated the knowledge with anything that had to do with the building of a social argument or a moral* argument?

2) Go to the library to further understand the previous or following reference if you need to and explain specifically what new information you acquired from what source(s).

or

3) Choose any one of Greene's textual references (in chapters 2, 3, or 4) that interests you but that you don't have enough specific background to understand. Use the library or a person knowledgeable about that subject to get the understanding you need. Then explain how that new knowledge makes possible the understanding of the argument she is constructing. Show how the new knowledge enables you to connect this reference with her use of a previous reference or following reference.

Notes: It is fine with me for you to work with another student in the class and for the two of you to "swap knowledge." If you choose this method, please record the process in your journals.

* Let's talk about what "moral" means in this context.

In class discussion following this assignment some elementary education students and practicing elementary teachers have talked openly about seeing themselves as people who understand children but not necessarily complex texts that interpret historical and social realities. One student raised the possibility of her own defensive identification with children against what she perceived as baffling books. Some students reported enjoying Greene's text tremendously, were familiar with many of her citations, and found the assignment intriguing. Others spoke of the relief of coming to know (as a result of the particular work they chose to do related to the assignment) a classic that she cited which they always felt that they should have known. A few students reported finding the text unnecessarily dense, therefore making it difficult to isolate one particular citation's relationship to another.

The range of responses has led me to take more seriously the need to accommodate different capacities to absorb social foundations knowledge, by balancing in the same course difficult theoretical texts like *The Dialectic of Freedom* with carefully selected memoir and imaginative literature. The strategy then is to approach the memoir or imaginative literature in such a way as to make explicit how the critical social theory we have studied plays out in the life of one person or in the lives of the limited constellation of characters in one memoir or selection of imaginative literature. This is what I conceive of as using *life-text* to show how people's lives illustrate embodied theory. (Chapter 5 includes an example of such work in the context of the course Social Action as Curriculum.)

Our students need lots of practice with the concept of social construction of identity, morality, and knowledge. But again, such experiences with interpretation have the advantage of initiating the intellectual stretch in the very place where elementary education students and teachers have proven strongest, that is, their genuine interest in the life experience of other people.

Another strategy is to continually link our in-class assignments with what our students are doing with children. Offering them support to assimilate difficult texts needs to be explicitly connected with the supports they will need to provide for the children in their classrooms. Parallel to what's necessary in our work with our students, our students need to move beyond a mechanical skills-focused approach to teaching text with the children in their own classrooms. For example, they might need to challenge themselves in a classroom where intellectual facilitation of child-led activity has been too passive. Julia Weber Gordon's *My Country School Diary* offers particularly fine modeling of critically self-reflective and intellectually active teaching and has proven as fine a "companion text" to *The Dialectic of Freedom* as to *The School and Society The Child and the Curriculum*. Together, the three texts invite the use of diverse selections from children's literature to offer our students practice · with deconstructing aspects of the social and psychological construction of the characters with the children they will teach.

The "lessons" of these study guides and assignments for the broader picture of our work

My hope here is to contribute to the continuing dialogue about pedagogical practices in teacher education programs committed to promoting social justice. Of specific interest to me is expanding the range of approaches to foundational education, particularly for elementary teachers and students. At present, we need a concerted effort to contradict the inappropriate expectations that have prevailed in the field about the ability of elementary educators to think in complex ways about social issues. When we introduce spiritualized conceptions of what it is possible to do, like "seize the dialectic of freedom," model a "wholeness of labor," and offer the perspective that people's life stories *are* the stuff of history, literature, and all other arts, we not only provide access to complex thinking, but we also reinforce the parallel practice implications of this work for our students' work with children in public school classrooms.

The integration of thinking and doing advocated for in the lessons featured in this chapter have implications for the way we go about organizing and doing the work of elementary teacher education more generally as well. We need to challenge the historic separation in education departments of the teaching of foundations courses (social, cultural, and political) from the supervision of our students' fieldwork. We need to rethink our departments' typical isolation from the liberal arts schools of our universities, where students of color in particular tend to perceive those of us in education as the gatekeepers for the dominant culture. At the same time, we will need to expand the range of fieldwork available to our students to provide experiences with diverse communities that are less—or differently—constricted than experiences we can help make available through public schools.

How *The Dialectic of Freedom* affected the content of this book

It was actually in (dialectical) response to the teaching experiences described in this chapter that I collaborated with students and community members to develop the course Social Action as Curriculum. This course provides a more appropriate context for the teaching of social reconstructionist text because it requires students to enact their own interpretation of the dialectic of freedom in collaboration with others in the local community. (See Chapter 5.)

The collaboration involved in developing the course speaks very specifically to the exciting possibilities that emerge from a commitment to enacting both the "wholeness of labor" and the "dialectic of freedom" for elementary education. In addition to a new immigrant artist, a small group of graduate students including four from elementary education and six from other programs and departments, the local African American minister, Reverend Henry J. Ausbey, whose poem is featured in the next chapter, was a key player in the initial experiment of this course. He provided us wonderful vitality and enthusiasm for our project as well as important connections to local new immigrant communities. Reverend Ausbey also contributed his own poetry to the mural project that became the activist focus of this first experience of the course. That contribution activated a "dialectic of freedom" for the project, resulting in the decoupage of three other poems, one written in Arabic, into the mural. The mural itself was collaboratively negotiated and painted by my students and one hundred fifty mostly new immigrant residents of a local housing authority complex where the Saratoga Cultural Histories Mural still lives, undefaced.

The next chapter represents my vision of elementary classrooms where the dialectic of freedom is in continual operation. But I want to end this chapter by reaffirming my belief that the dialectic of freedom is a spiritual concept and that Dewey's opposition to the division of labor is a spiritual stance. Both serve to remind me of Ruddick's proposition that we have lives of our own, but they are inextricably connected to others. I convey to my students my belief in the spirituality of the above conceptions through both my privileged authority as a professor, and the personal passion behind my commitment to social justice, which I also interpret as a spiritual phenomenon.

Chapter Three
A Day in the Life of Social Reconstructionist Arts-Based Teaching on a Multi-age Elementary Team:
Parallel Practices for the Elementary School Classroom

This chapter takes the reader on a journey into the life of two adjoining multi-age classrooms, one primary (first through third grade) and the other upper elementary (fourth through sixth grade) in a public urban socially diverse elementary school. The classrooms are unusual in their vision of a coherent first through sixth grade curriculum that inspires appropriately challenging work for all of the children, including the oldest and youngest; indeed the teamed teachers enjoy a continual collaborative relationship around a shared commitment to an integrated arts-based curriculum.

Selected vignettes and descriptive summaries focused on specific lessons and activities in both classrooms during one day of this teaching team's ongoing "urban-rural" unit will reflect an expansive interpretation of "inclusive" classrooms. Related, the reader will be presented with evidence that the commitment to arts integration as the motor of the curriculum is both inspired by and makes possible the enactment of such an expansive conception of inclusion.

The adjoining multi-age primary first-through-third grade and upper elementary fourth-through-sixth grade classrooms whose collaborative "urban-rural" unit is explored anecdotally in this chapter represent a "best practices" composite. That is, the school, teachers, curriculum, and these specific adjoining classrooms, including the children and their families and the multiple communities to which they belong, are based on my own teaching, research, and observations of "best practices" in a wide range of classrooms and community arts projects over many years.

Five broad organizing principles of the classrooms

I have identified five broad principles that organize and/or characterize the life of both classrooms. For the purposes of this narrative-based research they will also serve to organize this chapter:

1) The featured teaching team relies on the families of the children in the classroom and members of the communities that circumscribe the school, both for teaching artists who can collaborate with them as curriculum-makers, and for creative, humanistic, and artistic inspiration for the curriculum in general. Further, the team is assertive about finding and using the arts resources available in the community.

2) Morning meeting is a business meeting where all parties concerned help to organize the day and clarify expectations. Issues of appropriate behavior are negotiated in a manner that re-sets the tone each morning; the point is for children to be attentive enough to enjoy the fruits of this exciting curriculum, to not "miss out" because they have allowed themselves to become distracted from the important and gratifying business at hand.

3) Specific artistic techniques and challenging historical information are taught to the children, giving them the tools to enrich their independent work and create high-quality and therefore gratifying written, graphic, and plastic (three-dimensional) products.

4) Constant blocks of time are provided for play and independent exploration of the rich resources available. "Products" of play and independent exploration periods are prominently displayed in the classroom and efforts are consistently made to spiral curriculum from interesting pursuits of the children initiated during these blocks of time.

5)   Not necessarily predictable classroom incidents and accidents
      are used to spiral curriculum. In other words, the need to
      respond appropriately to real and interesting occurrences, cer-
      tainly part of what gives life meaning, becomes the context
      for further learning. Even events of systematic instruction in
      these classrooms acquire a "response to . . ." context that makes
      them compelling.

Organization of this chapter

The bulk of this chapter is organized into five sections, each correlated with one of the five broad principles identified above. In turn,
each of these principles is used to place specific aspects of the rich
curriculum of the two classrooms in a highly pragmatic context. At
least one vignette or description centered on curriculum or the negotiation of behavioral norms is offered to concretize the principle's
implications for classroom practice. Yet the broad principles provide an accessible link between the curriculum itself and the theory
that grounds my (and the featured teaching team's) appreciation of
that curriculum. Therefore, theoretical discussion and/or interpretation that speaks to both the vignettes and the highlighted principle of each section is typically labeled and set apart from the
vignette for the reader's ease. Occasionally such discussion is more
seamlessly woven into the content of the vignette, reminding the
reader that thoughtful teaching represents the continual enactment
of the teachers' best response (informed by theory) to what happens in the classroom and the communities in which it is situated.
In turn, such thoughtful response can generate new theory.

It is clear that some of the vignettes correlate equally well with
more than one principle; in some cases my matches may feel arbitrary. Yet the ease with which the curriculum can be correlated to
multiple principles might be seen as an argument for the cohesive-
ness and thoughtfulness of all aspects of classroom life.

An introduction to the featured teaching team and its general
guiding perspectives/philosophy follows below and immediately

precedes the five sections. After the five sections a brief conclusion summarizes the chapter's content with an emphasis on the transferability of its "lessons."

Social reconstructionism as guiding philosophy

The perspective of the featured teaching team is that the arts are about creating or making things happen in response to interpreted experiences of life in community. But the community cited in the definition, both practically and theoretically, represents many communities. It includes the actual families of the children in these classrooms and the multiple communities to which they belong ethnically, geographically, historically, and geo-politically. Whenever possible, these communities are invited to be active players in the curriculum.

The practices of the teaching team confirm the belief of its members in "social reconstructionist" teaching. Although related to "constructivism," "social reconstructionism" is the philosophy that grounds the educative project of reconstructing society to make it socially equitable (Kliebard, 1987; Sleeter, 1999). The curriculum of social reconstructionist classrooms, then, is characterized by intentionality with regard to the selection and passing on to learners of knowledge considered useful and important by communities interested in challenging social inequities and promoting democracy. Such knowledge then becomes the basis for experiential learning in the classroom and local community as part of a process of reconstructing the cultural worlds of the school community and the communities that circumscribe it; this reconstructive process is deemed the goal of education. Some of the vignettes in the chapter should illustrate for readers how the relationship of mutual responsibility between the classrooms and these overlapping communities helps this teaching team determine what to teach and how and to whom to teach it. In the two featured classrooms it is assumed that the children, often in collaboration with one another and their teachers, parents, and community members, will generate new understandings in response to knowledge made available both through text and experience. Both the knowledge presented and the new understandings take the form of some combination of language, graphic, music, culinary, plastic, or building arts.

Interestingly, classrooms with strongly arts-focused curriculum can provide unique data with regard to a continual balance between constructivist practices and systematic instruction that social reconstructionism requires, precisely because the curriculum keeps demanding creation, and therefore obviates those underlying skills and knowledge bases required to make very different creative acts possible. Although some children learn this knowledge and these skills through the interpretive and creative activities themselves, the overwhelming majority of children need systematic instruction in some areas, some of the time.

Therefore, the classrooms are guided by the belief that certain skills and some previous knowledge are always required in order to understand and produce interpretation; this belief is both observable and explicitly stated. Members of the teaching team articulate with and for the children the (loose) division of much of the work they pursue together into the categories "practice for . . ." and "the real thing." "The real thing" includes the work of understanding, interpreting, and creating, while "practice for . . ." generally applies to phonetic decoding skills, math facts and formulas, including skills with measurement, research and study skills, procedural knowledge with regard to use of art and science materials, and information deemed useful to memorize or "know." Sometimes this last category includes the historical background to appreciate a particular art form or innovation or to understand how some idea "became thinkable."

Often, but not always, "systematic instruction" supports the sequential building of a set of skills and therefore correlates with the "practice for" category, in that these sometimes sequentially acquired skills are required in order to pursue analytic, interpretive and creative work, but in and of themselves, do not constitute analytic, interpretive, or creative work. Yet the reader will hopefully appreciate that in these classrooms aspects of the process by which children are given access to artistic texts of all types—graphic, literate, visual, and plastic—can be both systematic and constructivist. The sometime fluidity of these categories will be explored further in the discussions that examine more deeply the practice implications of each of the five principles.

Reality principle number one:
The featured teaching team relies on the families
of the children in the classroom and members of
the communities that circumscribe the school . . .

COTTON PICKIN' TIME

Early, Early on Saturday Morning
Ever so slowly I climb out of bed
Find myself a string to hold up my britches
Make a newspaper hat to put on my head
Make my way into the Kitchen
Help myself to the syrup and bread.

Throw my daddy's old shirt on my back
Pull my raggedy sneakers upon my feet
getting myself ready to go to the cotton patch
Gotta help my mother make ends meet.

The big green truck pulls up to the door
Like sheep to the slaughter we all pile in
The family and me, everybody on the back!
To be driven to the fields where the pickin' will begin.

From sun up to sun down we'll labor
Row after row we'll pick
headache, finger ache, back ache, never mind
I ain't got time to be sick.

The grass still all wet with dew
Although its morning, there is yet no sun
And my legs get wet from my knees on down
Not exactly my idea of fun.

But the two bucks a day
   which will be my pay
      Gotta go along way.

So I get used to it. Its no big deal
That's the way it is. I don't complain
It's not blood!
Besides before this day is over. It'll be so hot
I'll be wishing for that dew. And praying for rain
or a flood.

'Cause when them cotton bows get open
And I ain't got a dime
It don't matter about the weather
For me, it's Cotton Pickin' Time!

                    Henry J. Ausbey

Vignette #1: Tuesday morning before school

It is 7:45 A.M., and eight-year-old Luis has returned from the main office to his multi-age primary classroom carrying forty copies of the above poem. Two of Luis's teachers, Mrs. D. and Ms. R., greet both Luis and the poem with enthusiasm. The poem was written by a local African American minister, Reverend Ausbey, when he was sixteen years old about his experience at that time growing up as son of a Mississippi sharecropper. Now a clergyman-activist in this medium-sized New York State Southern Tier city, Reverend Ausbey is the minister of Luis's family's small Haitian congregation and an advocate in this historic refugee resettlement area for new immigrant families, many of whose children, like Luis, attend this high-poverty public urban elementary school.

The consulting special education teacher in Luis's classroom, Ms. R., had recently attended the "Opening" for the Saratoga Cultural Histories Mural featuring Reverend Ausbey's poem at a municipal housing authority residence where Luis's family lives, less than a mile from school. The mural was a project of the elementary teacher education program from which Ms. R. graduated, and she and her team regularly sponsored student teachers.

Knowing that Luis's family attended the small Haitian congregation to which Reverend Ausbey ministered, and that Luis's entire extended family had attended the mural opening, Ms. R. had arranged during a regular parent conference last week which included herself, his regular classroom teacher Mrs. D., Luis, both of his parents and his grandmother, that Luis would request permission from Reverend Ausbey to copy the poem for use in their team's current "urban-rural" unit. It was also agreed at that conference that Luis would have the poem duplicated in the office (this morning) as part of his before-school-helper assignment, a job held at least once during each school term by every child on this elementary team.

After Ms. R., Mrs. D. and Luis reached agreement to wait until morning meeting to distribute Reverend Ausbey's poem, the two teachers sent Luis next door to the multi-age upper elementary classroom, where he would continue his before-school-helper job. Here Luis works with Mr. G., the teaching assistant who divides his assignment between Luis's classroom and this one. Mr. G. and Luis begin unpacking and remounting on large collapsible foamboards the Lewis Hine photography exhibit, on loan from the Southern Tier Institute for the Arts in Education (STI), which Mr. G. picked up from the institute's downtown office on his way home from work the previous afternoon. (Lewis Hine was the early-twentieth-century photographer whose work exposed child labor practices while capturing aspects of the humanity of his subjects beyond their victimization.) Luis has experienced traveling exhibits before, and is able to follow Mr. G.'s instructions for sorting the eight-and-a-half-by-eleven-inch photographs according to their vertical or horizontal orientation in preparation for mounting them in the already prepared photo brackets glued to the foamboard. The two continue working to ready the exhibit for the children, who will be stepping off their buses shortly.

Mr. G. is a comfortable and well-loved adult in Luis's school life; just yesterday he had written the word "emergency" in Luis's personal wordbook while helping him and his friend Michael write a sign to identify the hospital in the city being built in the primary classroom block area. That drama related to the same "urban-rural" unit for which both Reverend Ausbey's poem and the photography exhibit are important resources. Luis's sign will appear in a later vignette.

Discussion: "Maternal thinking" and reconstruction of the "codes of the culture of power"

The artfulness of the arts-based curriculum is as visible in the relationships orchestrated by the teachers as in the actual curriculum created by collaboration among these players: children, teachers, poets, artists, and community activists. It is a classroom community whose teachers continually tell and model for the children that intellectual and social connection-making is the point. The teaching team, male and female members alike, recognize the commitment that, historically, women have made as mothers as the prototype for their own elementary teaching. Such a paradigm invokes philosopher Sara Ruddick's conception of "maternal storytelling" (1989, pp. 97–101) to characterize the teachers' role in the teacher-student relationship.

> Ideally, a mother's stories are as beneficial to her children as they are to her. As she pieces her children's days together, a mother creates for herself and her children the confidence that the children have a life, very much their own and inextricably connected with others. (p. 98)

Thus, this team helps the children contextualize their own life experience in a hugely encompassing classroom community—one which pulls in the historical community of the area, the children's communities of family and friends, and ultimately, even the human community of "knowers" and artists. Ms. R. and Mr. G. literally tell Luis a story of his "inextricable connectedness" in the first vignette where Reverend Ausbey's poem introduces Luis and his classmates

to a potential inclusive identity as "poets" and the Lewis Hine photography exhibit reminds him/them that this country was built by
immigrants like himself. Reverend Ausbey is an African American
poet and Luis can become a Haitian American poet and one of the
poets in his classroom/school. Here is the enactment of an expanded
notion of the "codes of the culture of power," the tools that this
team agrees must be systematically taught to children of color and
other marginalized children in order for them to succeed in a culture whose "codes" are determined by a white and middle class
dominant culture. (Delpit, 1995) This teaching team includes poetry
as one such code while recognizing that poetry can be used to
include, even celebrate, all immigrant cultures and all people. In
this social reconstructionist classroom the "code" of poetry will be
"passed on" to the children; indeed, selections from Walt Whitman,
Langston Hughes, and Emily Dickinson grace the prominent bulletin board to which Reverend Ausbey's poem, and poems produced
by Luis and his classmates, will be added beginning this afternoon.
The code, "poetry," is transformed by the new contributions of this
community. It is literally reconstructed by the additions to the bulletin board of "Cotton Pickin' Time" and then by poems produced
by the children in the poetry workshop convened this morning by
Mr. G. and in turn by the children themselves (captured in the next
vignette).

Vignette #2: Poetry workshop after group meeting

Mr. G. works with eight children immediately after group meeting,
six from the primary classroom and two from upper elementary.
Charles, an eleven-year-old, volunteers to read aloud "Cotton
Pickin' Time" for this self-selected group of poets whose primary
members have already heard it read by Luis earlier in group meeting. Mr. G. then reiterates what the group has come together for:
writing poetry about rural work. In the brief introductory discussion he facilitates, the children are reminded and remind one another
of some of their most recent sources of information about rural work:

Last Friday, Mr. Estavez, a former migrant apple picker from Wayne County, New York, had visited both classrooms and shared oral histories from his crew (compiled through a grant from the Cornell Migrant Program, whose director is a friend of Mrs. D.'s). Yesterday, Mrs. D. had read to the primary group the picture book, *A Green Horn Blowing* (Birchman, 1997), an imaginative Depression-era tale narrated in the first person by an unnamed young boy living on his aunt's farm. The story featured an itinerant farmworker, John Potts, who temporarily came to do odd farm jobs and live in Aunt Frita's barn with the cats. But John Potts was also a skilled trumpet-player, and he discovered for the narrator a fantastic playable green squash called the *trombolia*. That book, although a joyful fantasy, had reinvoked the conversation sparked by Mr. Estavez's presentation in which he had pointed out the low pay of farmworkers and their special vulnerability in times of economic crisis. With Mr. G.'s recursive questioning, Charles recalled that Mr. Estavez was particularly passionate about one point: those who helped ensure that all of us could eat deserved to feel secure about their own ability to provide good food and shelter for their families. Luis pointed out that although John Potts made beautiful music, and worked hard on Aunt Frita's farm, he had no security about his next meal or his next bed, even for himself alone.

Two younger children mentioned Mr. G.'s stories about baling hay on his grandparents' farm in Iowa. And two other children were reminded that their families bought corn from a farmstand only ten minutes outside the city; one of the children knew a boy from this school who worked at the stand selling corn in the summer. Aveen spoke of her grandfather's farm in New Jersey which she loved to visit; her grandfather grew corn but earned most of his income training horses.

The above discussion segues into Mr. G.'s explanation of the specific lesson plan. He asks the children to listen for characteristics of the language or ideas as he rereads Reverend Ausbey's poem. He identifies specific choices the poet made in the writing of "Cotton Pickin' Time" as "variables." Again, through recursive questioning he has the children identify some of these variables. The children name the presence of rhyming words, the use of informal, family and community-based language (sometimes called without derogatory connotations "street language" in these classrooms), images related to the realities of "making ends meet," and the use of details of ordinary life, like the specifics of getting dressed and eating bread with syrup. When it is her turn as leader, nine-year-old Aveen selects rhyme and a description of someone eating as the two variables to which the children's poems must conform this round.

Discussion: Categories of teaching practices blur

This anecdote provides an example of the blurring of categories, "systematic instruction" and "constructivist practices," as well as the teachers' informal categories for use with the children "practice for . . ." and "the real thing." For instance, the generating of a list of words that rhyme with "corn" could be part of a lesson representing systematic instruction in mechanical decoding and encoding skills. In that case, it would represent the category "practice for . . ." Yet the generating of such a list might also be part of a poetry-writing lesson in which students are being encouraged to play with and produce rhymed verse in the context of an exploration of rural work, as is the case in this poetry workshop.

The organization and facilitation of the poetry workshop itself, though, also invokes questions of what is "real" and what is "practice." Through Mr. G.'s facilitation, children are reminded of the very "real" proposition of Sara Ruddick's that they have "a life very much their own and inextricably connected with others"—others like Reverend Ausbey and their teachers and even John Potts with his fantastic *trombolia*. Nine-year-old Aveen wants to experiment with rhyme and has an idea for a poem of her own that features the hot water without tea that her grandma drank as a new young mother in a village in Kurdistan. For Aveen, the writing of this poem will be very "real," as is her experience facilitating the workshop as a "practice" teacher. And for the other children in the group writing poems following Aveen's specifications, will the experience represent "the real thing" or "practice for . . ." ? It's unclear. But isn't it quite systematic to identify the different ways a poem "means" (Ciardi, 1959) as "variables" and to have children selecting and assigning them for use by the community of poets in their classroom?

Reality principle number two:
Morning meeting is a business meeting where all parties
concerned help to organize the day and clarify expectations

Vignette #3: Simultaneous group meetings

Two morning meetings proceed simultaneously in the younger and older elementary classrooms. Much of what will unfold during the day, including, for instance, Mr. G.'s poetry workshop described above and the use by the children of the Lewis Hine exhibit, are introduced in these parallel morning meetings. The younger children will receive a copy of and hear Luis introduce and read Reverend Ausbey's poem. The older children will receive their first pictures taken on a recent downtown field trip, developed by Dounya's dad, Bosnian immigrant photographer Sead Hadziabdic. Mrs. H. reminds the older children that most of them will have the opportunity to study the Lewis Hine exhibit and to plan their individual and small group multi-media research projects related to the "urban-rural" unit. Some of them will be participating in groups that directly support some aspect of their research. In both classrooms children are reminded that because Mr. Hadziabdic will return this afternoon for a workshop on lighting with the upper elementary children, math instruction groups will convene this morning after snack. Mrs. H. has arranged to meet with children working with unifix on multiplication towers in the downstairs resource room again, as that room is equipped with many more unifix cubes than the classrooms.

In the primary classroom the participants of this morning's watercolor group with primary teacher Mrs. D. identify themselves, as do the cooks working with parent volunteer Debra to produce the applesauce and accompanying flyer for tonight's PTA meeting. Members of the cross-team writing support group are reminded of their regularly scheduled meeting with consulting special education teacher Ms. R. in the upper elementary classroom directly following this one. The odyssey math team involving one primary and seven upper elementary students, including eleven-year-old Thomas, who has severe cerebral palsy, will meet with nine-year-old student captain Dinesha and Ms. S., classroom aide assigned to Thomas, out in the hall to continue plotting the scale and provisional plan for the model city construction project to begin tomorrow in the upper elementary art area. Thomas will manipulate materials and enthusiastically cheerlead for the other children. Ms. S. will also brainstorm with the students how they plan to individualize the model city project into their own "urban-rural" research project. And in both meetings teachers restate the authentic recording requirement. Every student must "leave a trace" in the form of a written or graphic chronicling of some activity they performed during the day.

In the primary classroom, examples are offered this morning as every morning to clarify what will be considered acceptable chronicling. Will the leaflet "count" for the children in Debra's group? "Yes!" Will poems produced in Mr. G.'s group "count"? If you are working on the unifix tower problems, can you write up your process solving one of the problems with words? "Yes!" Can you illustrate a problem with a diagram? "Yes, but only if it's detailed enough!" Can Michael do a blockstory or diagram with Luis about the emergency room of the hospital? "Yes!" (Luis feels obligated to point out that he will be working with Mr. G.'s poetry group first thing.) Mr. T. offers that he'll be with Michael in blocks. Might he help Michael write such a story, possibly including the other children who are starting the morning there? Michael is clearly delighted to have Mr. T.'s shared attention connect him to the two other children who plan to work in blocks.

Discussion: The artfulness of navigating group meeting

All teachers can appreciate how the best intentions with regard to curriculum-making can be sabotaged by lack of cooperation on the part of the children, or even the "acting out" of a few children. Arts-focused social reconstructionist teaching requires the full engagement of the children as a community. Yet the process of achieving such engagement is an artform in itself. While the long-term goal is to have a curriculum that continually spirals from the preceding inquiry, creative project, or other work of individual and small groups of children, in reality, there are constant compromises required by both state-mandated curriculum and inevitable contradictory school and community expectations. Then there is the issue of differences in skill level and background information on the part of individual children, requiring different amounts of, and/or different timing in the provision for, systematic instruction. These realities help explain why the teachers call the first block after morning meeting "assigned morning activity time" even though more than half of the children are typically working in a teacher-facilitated group whose initiation or content the children themselves helped negotiate. Afternoon "independent work time" allows similar flexibility for teacher direction, and both "writing workshop" and whole and small-group "math instruction" are typically teacher-directed. All of these blocks are regularly scheduled, some daily and some bi- or tri-weekly. The children know that only blocks specifically labeled "play and independent exploration" are consistently "free choice."

Clearly then, assigning activities and confirming ongoing commitments and choices in morning meeting proceeds conversationally and involves a great deal of negotiation. It requires a kind of maturity and patience that some of the children find too challenging without assistance. Yet assistance comes in many forms, not typically requiring one-to-one aides. For instance, Mrs. D. has a gift for successfully reinforcing behavioral expectations in light and humorous interactions that are consistent with the social reconstructionist philosophy. Two such interactions are featured in the following vignettes.

Vignette #4: Larry in primary group meeting

Larry is a seven year old who generally functions well in the primary classroom. He arrived from another school in the fall with a five-inch-thick folder, mostly documenting his "behavioral challenges" and "emotional problems."

Before the assignment and selection of activities, Mrs. D. announces lunch-count. "[She] need[s] every child's attention to complete this process without wasting too much of the morning's assigned activity time. If everybody hears all the lunch choices the first time, they can be prepared to make their selections in one round," Mrs. D. explains as she often does in morning meeting. But Larry is fooling around with a rubber band at Mrs. D.'s feet, trying to keep encircled a fast-moving spider. "I appreciate your gentleness with that spider, Larry. Do you think we could catch it in a cup and release it out the window?" Although many children volunteer, Mrs. D. encourages Larry to complete the job by himself as she hands him an empty coffee cup from the desk just behind her; she knows Larry well enough to know his skill in such matters; this interruption will not take long and it will bear long-term fruit. The children get reinforcement for an important rule in this community: we respect all living things. And Larry, at times annoying to the other children, is seen at his most gentle, kind, and thoughtful in this brief sequence of events. In post-structuralist terms, the situation, under Mrs. D.'s skillful guidance, "constructs" Larry as gentle, kind, and thoughtful.

And then there is the lovely quiet moment during which everyone watches Larry coax the spider off the rim of the cup held just outside the cracked-open window. Mrs. D. waits respectfully, modeling the awed silence she intentionally chooses to cultivate as a resource for this classroom where beautiful things are regularly observed and made. Larry completes the job and seats himself in his original place. But the children immediately surrounding him feel gifted now to have him in their midst. There is some shifting around of bottoms and legs to make room for him, yet somehow everyone is seated even closer to him than before. The child immediately behind him places his hand on Larry's back. With a rejecting movement, he shrugs off the hand. The spell is broken. Larry is a child who can't tolerate too much attention for a sweetness he can't maintain.

Mrs. D. returns to the first agenda of the meeting: lunch-count. But she will bring a kind of closure to the Larry incident, recognizing the need to welcome him back as the Larry who is not always so gentle, not always so appropriate. She accomplishes this with an almost offhand wry remark, made with her head turned to the board and chalk in hand, ready to write the egg noodle casserole tally. The comment she makes is directed to the more cynical side of Larry, the side of him that has seen a bit too much in his fairly chaotic life outside of school. "There must be an oversupply of those noodles this week, Larry, because they're certainly appearing regularly on this week's lunch menus," she comments. "There was a special at the warehouse, huh, Mrs. D.," says Larry, now grinning. He's a child who already knows that the school nurse would be hard pressed to count ketchup as a vegetable. The hand of the boy behind him replaces itself on Larry's back and this time it is not shrugged off.

Her comment represents Mrs. D.'s very personal approach to keeping Larry sufficiently connected to her, to the other children, and to the complex agenda of this exciting classroom. He cannot be a gentle "good boy" much of the time; it is too great a contradiction with his life outside of school where he is being raised by a single often well-intentioned but "macho" father living in poverty. (Just two days ago Mrs. D. had interrupted Larry's gleeful narration of his witnessing his father throw a brick through his girlfriend's car window.) But this classroom will offer Larry many opportunities to do and be both gentle and good. Mrs. D.'s comment about the oversupply of noodles lets him and the other children know that there is space here for Larry in all his complexity. This includes the Larry that knows too much, including the potential hypocrisy of adults, even around their voiced concerns about children's nutritional needs.

Discussion: Theorizing a relationship between social reconstructionism and behavioral norms

The point is that social reconstructionist teaching includes the reconstruction of all of the players, including the children. Larry's goodness gets stretched further in the above sequence of events, just as his harder edge gets softened a bit because Mrs. D.'s noodle comment is not rude or inappropriate, just aware in the way Larry is. One could argue, relative to the focus of this chapter, that there is an artful approach to inclusion modeled here. Children are reshaped and reshape themselves in order to fit into this humane and expansive community.

But I would be remiss in not articulating what most teachers certainly appreciate: the reality that economic, social, and cultural factors combined with individual psychological dynamics do not explain all behavior in a classroom, and also that children's conflicts, regardless of their causes, can lead to significant disruption in any setting. It is important to note that children can reject physical contact for many reasons. Larry is not autistic, nor does he suffer from other neurological problems, but some children who behave similarly do. Most teachers are familiar with "tactile defensiveness" more serious than Larry's that sometimes appears in children who have been abused or have certain neurological problems. Increasingly, children with tactile defensiveness are "brushed" or otherwise offered desensitization treatments in school; for many of them, the consistent support of an aide with training is essential to their success.

As well, a teacher in Mrs. D.'s position could have just as realistically reminded the class about the need to ask permission before touching. Many teachers in active classrooms hold all meetings while children are seated at their desks or tables to minimize such complications. And sometimes it is important to give children appropriate information about the special needs of their peers. The point here is that there is always a balance between allowance for the raw data of life to play out for all of its educative potential, and the need to maintain the levels of order, confidentiality, and peace required by both the "players" and the complex, sometimes systematic curriculum.

Vignette #5: Lashanda in primary group meeting

Lashanda is a six year old whose family refused to have her "held back" in kindergarten, despite the strong recommendation of the school psychologist and kindergarten teacher, both of whom perceived her to be too immature for first grade. Although not always opposed to young children repeating kindergarten, this teaching team thinks Lashanda's family made a good decision.

After Mrs. D. has completed lunch-count, Ms. R. reviews the morning's group assignments and choices. She publicly welcomes Debra, a community volunteer who visits weekly to cook with a rotating group of children from both classrooms. Ms. R. reminds the children that Debra is here to help this week's cooks with the applesauce they are making for today's snack and for tonight's PTA meeting. The cooking group will also be responsible for completing the leaflet to be distributed at the PTA meeting, which will include, as has already been agreed, the recipe, the bisected apple diagram produced by Lashanda last Friday, and whatever else this week's group decides to include.

Lashanda is stimulated by the mention of her name and raises her hand. "Couldn't Reverend Ausbey's poem be included in the leaflet for the PTA too." In the conversation that ensues, a number of children restate the opinion that Reverend Ausbey's poem "Cotton Pickin' Time" would not match the theme of the leaflet. Perhaps there would be time to produce a poem about applesauce-making, Mrs. D. suggests. "No, we'll make the recipe rhyme," counters a child sitting next to Lashanda. Debra is as visibly delighted as a couple of the "cooks" who now gaze at Lashanda with new admiration.

Discussion: More "child-shaping"

Again, there is a kind of subtle shaping of a child into gradually more responsible community membership. Lashanda's "immaturity" sometimes takes the form of needing to talk even when she doesn't really have something compelling to say. In classrooms that invite student input, this common pattern can become a problem. But Lashanda is a natural connection-maker; she proposes a connection that is not quite direct enough "to make sense" to this community but evidences her awareness that the point is this continual effort to make connections. And she is immediately rewarded by Mrs. D.'s modeling of the effort to work with her thinking and of another child's quick grasp of an exciting possible "compromise." The process of negotiating the curriculum itself, in this case, the creation of a rhyming applesauce recipe, is decidedly constructivist.

**Reality principle number three:
Specific artistic techniques are taught to the children,
giving them the tools to enrich their independent work
and create high-quality, and therefore gratifying, products**

Vignette #6: Watercoloring the sky

Students who experiment with the combination of blue watercolor, water, white paper, and masking gum are learning by "practice" how to represent the sky. Indeed, this is the immediate goal of the group that works with Mrs. D., who does watercolor painting in her life outside of school. They are systematically instructed in a technique, a technique which represents knowledge worthy of being preserved and passed on, a technique that will make it possible for them to create convincing and very different kinds of skies. Yet the children's experimentation with the technique is part of an artistic/creative/literate response in this lesson where mostly six year olds, the youngest children, work with Mrs. D. to create the sky in pictures for their book comparing urban and rural environments.

Later this afternoon during independent work time following writing workshop, they will use a combination of drawing and collage materials to continue crafting their pictures, inspired by research in books, films shown to the class, two field trips, another community artist and the Lewis Hine exhibit. Then, too, their completed pictures will finally require the children's own captions, produced in a series of writing workshops where the same children will use a combination of methods to re-represent in words the meaning they make of their graphic representations. Such methods include dictating to an adult or older child who does the actual writing, requesting words to be written in their wordbooks and transcribing them onto the book page, and "sounding out" the whole caption.

So this lesson represents a constructivist response to a number of different encounters with professional art even during this one day: the children have briefly viewed the Lewis Hine exhibit next door at the beginning of this lesson, being asked to focus only on the way "sky" appears in the photos during this first encounter. Also, available for their perusal on a display shelf adjoining their current painting workshop space in the primary classroom are a number of books that feature skies, including the beautifully illustrated children's picture book read yesterday morning in group meeting, *A Green Horn Blowing*, the rural Depression-era fantasy. Mrs. D. reminds them of Luis's reading of "Cotton Pickin' Time" in group meeting. Can they imagine the sky not described in the poem? A child points out that the day is very hot. "We know the sun must be a ball of fire," she adds. This afternoon the children will briefly visit next door to examine the foreboding sky in a famous photograph taken by Dounya's dad, Sead Hadziabdic. Do the children's opportunities to "research skies" represent events of systematic instruction because they lead to the children's ability to make their own sky pictures? Are these research opportunities a "practice for . . ." or "the real thing"? Or is no separation of categories possible in some of the complex constructivist events that constitute the core of this arts-based curriculum?

Discussion: Introduction to photography workshop

Certainly the same questions arise in the case of the activities related to the upper elementary classroom featuring the Lewis Hine photography exhibit. The study of the Lewis Hine photographs, capturing the lives of poor and working-class new immigrants including children to New York City at the beginning of the twentieth century, is central to the current "urban-rural" unit. As part of that unit, pursued at different levels of academic and intellectual challenge for different children in the two classrooms, all of the children have been given re-usable black-and-white cameras provided for by a grant through the local Roberson Museum's partnership with a number of classrooms in the local school district. Some of the older children are doing their research in the form of photo essays about urban work. Some will correlate research with their work on the model city project. Others will use poetry, including their own, to explore their choice of themes. Some photography will be a part of every project.

This afternoon, the older children prepare to take their own photographs in workshops where they learn from a visiting parent photographer not only how to operate the camera, but how Lewis Hine captured different qualities of the urban immigrant experience in his photographs.

Vignette #7: A parent's photography workshop
and a teacher's lectures

Mrs. H. welcomes Dounya's dad, Sead Hadziabdic, well known to the upper-elementary children, and delivers the good news that in the future, they will be developing their own pictures in the temporary darkroom Mr. Hadziabdic will be setting up in the storage closet. Dounya is proud to announce that her dad has been awarded the small decentralization grant from the New York State Council on the Arts that will fund his work with the children in the darkroom. Mrs. H. had written the grant with the input of Mr.

Hadziabdic and the editing help of three of the older children in two special afterschool meetings.

This afternoon, Sead Hadziabdic focuses on how the use of lighting contributed to the mood of heaviness and oppression conveyed in many of Lewis Hine's photographs. He shows the children his own award-winning photograph of the bridge at Mostar, taken by him just days before it was destroyed in a bombing during the war in Bosnia, and explains the choices he himself made about lighting. He emphasizes with the children the variables over which they have control with their own black-and-white cameras before they proceed outside to experiment with these variables.

Discussion: Photography, maternal storytelling, and "the codes"

In the course of his work with them Sead Hadziabdic articulates another "maternal story": that understanding the use of light is part of the knowledge base of the community of "inextricably connected" artists who call themselves photographers. It is a community that includes himself, with his desire to capture for the human community a gorgeous and important piece of architecture from his own and Dounya's own former homeland, and Lewis Hine, who likewise wanted the world to know about the exploitation of immigrant workers, including children. But it potentially includes as well the children in this classroom, who can also produce pictures of aspects of life they want to capture and share, should they choose to master the required skills.

In addition to the background information about the Lewis Hine photographs offered by Sead Hadziabdic, Mrs. H. has been giving brief mini-lectures to the whole class about the turn-of-the-century urban immigrant experience, including how and for what political and humanitarian motivations Lewis Hine took his pictures. Her lectures are also inspiration and support for the upper elementary research projects. She would argue that her mini-lectures represent systematic instruction in that she is providing a gradually deepening background for examining different aspects of that historical era. Does this work represent "practice for . . ." or the "real thing"?

For instance, a number of children have chosen to do their research in the form of a collective photo-essay about the history of work in the local area since the beginning of the twentieth century. Mrs. H. has introduced the concept of exploitation of the labor of new immigrants including children. And ten-year-old Catherine has decided to focus her research on the famous New York City newsboys' strike. Does Catherine's experience of Mrs. H.'s mini-lecture represents "practice for . . ." or "the real thing" in terms of a learning experience? Yet, what could be more "real" than the challenging historical-materialist information being "passed on" by Mrs. H.?

Discussion: Theorizing the writing support group

Following group meeting five children, three from primary and two from the upper elementary classroom, convene for writing support group with Ms. R. This is a group half of whose members have remained constant this school year and half of whom move in and out of the group. Membership is negotiated among teachers, families, and children, but the idea of a writing support group came out of the ongoing school-wide faculty research seminar, of which Mrs. H., Mrs. D., Ms. R., and Mr. G. are members. For a few months the previous year the seminar considered the needs of children who for various reasons and at different times resisted the group editing processes that were a standard component of writing workshop in a number of the classrooms in this school, including the two classrooms featured in this chapter.

Last year the faculty research seminar read both Anne Haas Dyson's *Social Worlds of Children Learning to Write in an Urban Primary School* (1993) and Elizabeth Ellsworth's "Why Doesn't This Feel Empowering?" (1989). Faculty members designed teacher action research projects related to inquiries potentially illuminated by either or both texts. These projects affirmed that the questions raised by

Dyson about a specific homeless child featured in her research resonated with the experience of a number of teachers in this school, including those on this teaching team. At various times a few children seemed too fragile to tolerate questions about their intentions and meaning relative to a written or performance piece. Ellsworth's article introduced to the teachers African American writer Barbara Christian's conception that she was "writing to save her own life." Mrs. D. realized how well that characterization periodically applied to some of the children in the classroom. Like Christian, they voiced experience that had not "figured in" to the dominant culture's conceptions of worthy human realities. They wrote to "save" their own lives by making them real. Their views could not be validated by others with no understanding of their experience. Parallel to Christian's argument about her writing on the realities of the lives of African American women writers, some of the written and performance pieces that these children created needed to be appreciated as a unique source of information. Such an interpretation did not invalidate the need for these children to learn the "codes of the culture of power," including conventional English grammar and syntax. However, the more public editing process through which skills were taught and reinforced with the students' own writing used as object (a process which, therefore, objectifies that writing to some extent) did not always feel safe. The writing support group, then, could serve two functions. It could provide a more selective audience for certain more sensitive written, graphic, and performance pieces. And it could provide a place to systematically teach conventional English syntax, grammar, and spelling skills ("codework") using a combination of materials other than the students' own writing. These materials included older linguistic readers, "Glass Analysis" (Glass, 1973) techniques similar to methods of reading recovery (Clay, 1985), and selected work of published poets and writers.

The faculty research seminar's findings above continued to influence the practices of the teachers on this team outside of the writing support group. For instance, the teachers in both classrooms tended to use what they articulated as "discoveries" made in writing support group for whole group and small group lessons that isolated a particular "decoding trick" or "encoding trick." And all of the children on this team continually wore a personal wordbook, attached to a belt or necklace like the one in which Mr. G. (yesterday) copied for Luis the word "emergency" for use on his block area sign. The idea was that everyone was at all times an authentic chronicler and poet, needing access to the words that could be "given" by anybody in the school (or wider community) who could spell them. You collected words like you collected life experience; some of the experience remained private or you only shared it with a carefully selected group. But words were always available to everyone for the giving and taking as both "practice for . . ." and "the real thing."

**Reality principle number four: Constant blocks
of time are provided for play and independent
exploration of the rich resources available to the children**

Vignette #8: The block area

With regard to the social reconstructionist philosophy that guides the curriculum, there is likewise continual interplay between the children's independent exploration, sometimes taking the form of play, and the creation of formal curriculum for the classroom. "Practice for . . ." and "the real thing" can take on somewhat different meanings, now reflecting the interpretation of "play" as "practice for" real life. In the context of building their city as part of the "urban-rural" unit, three of the younger children who spent part of the morning with Mr. T. in the block area also discovered how a pulley works. In their efforts to rig up an appropriately dramatic door for Luis and Michael's hospital emergency room, they were able to direct Mr. T. to attach a pulley arrangement to a hook already imbedded in the ceiling above the block area and to attach its string to the cardboard handle on that door.

Mrs. D.'s earlier group is now at the library checking out astronomy books for more sky inspiration. She walks over to the block area to help during the transitional time just before Mr. T. will be offering Michael one-to-one attention. Mr. T. suggests that the children read to Mrs. D. the story they have written, which turns out to focus on how they helped Mr. T. by taping and retaping the handle on the door to their hospital emergency room, finally discovering a way to get the cardboard attached to the pulley. She admires the detail and precise language they have used, and suggests that they share their story with the whole group before lunch.

As Michael leaves with Mr. T., Mrs. D. notices the elaborate and extremely tall clock tower at the center of their city. Would the two remaining children be interested in measuring their clock tower which Mrs. D. believes is the tallest structure built yet this year? The inquiry that ensues inspires in Mrs. D. her idea for a demonstration lesson in transition to standard measurement, which Mrs. D. will reconstruct with the two block-builders for the entire class during the next formal math instruction block. How many color cubes high is the tower? How many dog biscuits high? (This requires more taping and engenders much excitement. Dog biscuits had been introduced in math groups just yesterday afternoon, but they had measured only distances on the floor.) Not now, but in the formal group Mrs. D. will proceed to, "How many inches? How many centimeters?" The process of conversion to standard measurement is "systematic" in its movement from dog biscuits to color cubes to inches to centimeters. The children are engaged in "practice for" later work with standard measurement. And the skills of measurement will offer these children a background to begin to appreciate the more elaborate and scale-model city construction that the older children next door will begin tomorrow.

Yet the contextualization of the measurement lesson in their own work of city-building connects measurement to one of its very "real" locations in the world: a part of the knowledge base (even code) called "architecture." The same is the case with the story about the specific design of the pulley that controls the emergency room door. Indeed, the sharing of that story will spiral into an extensive study of pulleys and levers, integrating beautifully with the focus on inventions and technology that will naturally emerge during this "urban-rural" unit.

Vignette #9: Hattie and Sarah: Internet "surfing"

The controversies about use of the World Wide Web in classrooms like these are particularly "hot" at the present time. The teachers on this team continually discuss, argue, and compromise based on their different perspectives about the potential positive and negative effects of Internet use, even general computer use in school by the children, particularly in the context of the commitment to arts-based curriculum. Compromises have evolved on this team: both computers with Internet access are located in the upper elementary classroom, and there's a clearly articulated rule that children may only access bookmarked sites. However, bookmarked sites are many, varied, and fully available during "play and independent exploration blocks." Partly because of his own fascination with the intersections between computers and the arts, Mr. G. monitors computer use and continually bookmarks appropriate new finds.

Yesterday afternoon during a "free choice" time, twelve-year-olds Hattie and Sarah discovered one of Mr. G.'s newest finds from a university archive: a film clip about the minstrel show tradition from Marlon Riggs's *Ethnic Notions* in which Riggs himself portrays a famous African American singer of the early fifties removing the blackface makeup required of him in order to perform. Moved by this image, the girls proposed to Mrs. H. that their research project for the "urban-rural" unit take the form of an in-class museum installation they want to call "Artifacts of Slavery." This morning the girls brainstorm with Mrs. H. other ideas for their museum, eventually leading them to an Internet site featuring the manumission papers of slaves.

Discussion: Theorizing the in-classroom museum

This project of Hattie and Sarah's includes their own acquisition (a "passing on" to them) of a number of different kinds of knowledge: Internet access skills, the rich content and context of actual historical documents, and reinforcement that a concept of continual social change can help us organize and understand our worlds. In the context of these classrooms, the reality that artifacts represented separately in graphics and language can be unified for representation to others in museum installations, is a specifically practical lesson in interpretation that Hattie and Sarah have learned well, and now reinforce for the other children. And again, modeled for all of the children is reinforcement for their own invention of the curriculum of their classroom.

Reality principle number five:
Not necessarily predictable classroom
incidents are used to spiral curriculum

Discussion: Maternal thinking and the making of meaning in diverse classrooms

The practice of writing process has added much to the curriculum of elementary classrooms in recent years, including a renewed appreciation for using story—both telling and writing—to make sense of life experience in school. Especially significant for these classrooms is Sara Ruddick's (1989) contention that a mother's stories can help her children locate the meaning of their lives not just in their individual developing competence and independence but also in their connections to others. The subtle shift in perspective from the conventional view that mothers instill confidence so that children can successfully separate in order to achieve and fulfill themselves, to Ruddick's appreciation that mothers also instill confidence geared at helping children appreciate the importance of their connectedness to others, is the shift that makes her thinking so valuable to this social reconstructionist teaching team. For much of the social reconstructionist project is the revaluing of connection and community in the context of the increasingly global dominant culture that overvalues independence and autonomy.

As well, Ruddick's thinking is particularly intriguing in the context of teachers committed to critically facilitating meaning-making in public school classrooms with children from different social class and cultural backgrounds who have therefore suffered different kinds of social hurts. Especially now, a convergence of theory from diverse fields, including post-structuralist literary criticism and autobiographical/narrative inquiry, seems to confirm what many resourceful mothers have long understood: that self does not generate autobiographical memories. Rather the reverse is the case. In the words of co-researchers Craig Barclay and Rosemary Hodges, "The self is composed anew" in each presentation of autobiographical information (1990).

Those who study the effects of internalized oppression in themselves, in their students, and in an academic context understand that all internalized oppression causes feelings of social isolation. The potential to contradict feelings of social isolation in the classroom is certainly a strong motivation for teachers who believe that public schools can foster democracy.

Yet there is a problem with an uncritical understanding of "welcoming the child's home communities into the classroom" as paradigm for curriculum-making. Notwithstanding the appropriateness and richness of the connections Ms. R. helped forge among Luis, his Haitian community, Reverend Ausbey and poetry, and the comparably inspired curriculum-making involving the Bosnian refugee photographer Sead Hadziabdic, his own moving photograph, his daughter Dounya and the urban-rural unit, the reality is that for some children and their families, it is or feels unsafe for a child to reveal aspects of home life and family history in the classroom. While the most obvious situation is the potential revelation of illegal alien status, it is also the case that children of gay or lesbian families, children who have survived wars, children living in poverty, and children of non-dominant cultures can learn very quickly how unsafe the experience of revealing "lifestories" sometimes is or feels. Further, children who don't have this privilege of publicly connecting home and school experiences can shut down emotionally in classrooms that require a kind of boundary-lessness between the two communities.

Still, the inability to articulate the meaning of events in a community with a shared history can deprive children of what this teaching team defines as education. It is not just the joy of identification that is at stake; it is also the reality that group identification makes possible all acts of interpretation.

All of the above offers the rationale for principle number five, which recognizes the classroom itself as a real community in which things happen, many of them unpredictably. Spontaneous or unpredictable classroom events have a safe community-with-a-history context in which to explore their meaning. The classroom gives its members a shared history; events in its life can be safely chronicled and interpreted publicly by all, including children who have no other publicly safe communities. Related, children who have learned not to call attention to themselves or have learned to seek attention for negative behaviors for reasons including internalized oppression, can find a less threatening form of attention through their association among others with a funny or unexpected or otherwise meaningful classroom event.

Mrs. D. in particular has long understood the potential to help shape stronger "selves" through sensitive orchestration of autobiographical history generated right here in the classroom. She often seizes spontaneous classroom events as subject for the whole-group mini-lesson that typically precedes writing workshop. These mini-lessons usually represent events of systematic instruction, where a particular language arts skill is emphasized in each lesson. In the final two vignettes, such "instruction" is focused on both the skills of "being good reporters" and of "viewing events from multiple perspectives." But these vignettes are especially selected for placement at the end of this chapter because of their demonstration of the natural blurring of the categories of "systematic instruction," constructivism, "practice for . . ." and "the real thing" in effective arts-based social reconstructionist teaching. As an added bonus, by way of situating the reader with Larry when he had his accident, vignette #10 introduces to the reader the use of "the pinchpot lesson" (featured in Chapter 1 in the teacher education classroom) as an example of a historical-materialist social studies lesson suitable for all ages of children and adults, a useful resource in arts-based social reconstructionist teaching.

Vignette #10: Larry's accident

The subject of this afternoon's writing mini-lesson (which precedes writing workshop) requires some introduction. Today's lesson, "Seeing events from different perspectives," was a powerful social reconstructionist response to yesterday's "Being good reporters." And "Being good reporters" was in turn a collaboratively planned response to a classroom accident that happened the previous Friday, when Mr. G. was convening a group of clay pot–makers at the art table responding to the following assignment:

> Directions: You are a member of an early human community living by a clay-bottom river. You have realized for the first time the possibility of inventing "a container." Take your time creating this pot out of clay. When everyone in your group has a pot, come together for the following brainstorming activity: how is this discovery of the pot going to change the life of your community in both positive and negative ways?

The gist of the story, as it was dictated yesterday by the children one sentence each to Mrs. D. (writing furiously on her chart paper) was that Larry decided to use slab construction to build his pot and reasoned that he needed a heavy object with which to flatten his clay into a pancake. Although Mr. G. was present, Larry made his move to claim a large plastic jar of white paint from the supply crates behind him before Mr. G. looked up from his conversation with B., another child in the group. Larry immediately positioned the gallon container of white poster paint above his head and using all of his (notorious) physical force, slammed it down smack in the middle of a presently very flat clay pancake. However, the paint jar's previous user had been careless in screwing on the jar's lid. Larry, Mr. G., B., S., N., the art table, and much of the surface area of nearby walls and floors were suddenly plastered with thick dripping white paint.

Yesterday, Mrs. D. had probed for correct sequencing, details, exact quotes. As the story was orally reconstructed for her transcription into the classroom chronicle it became clear that the children had absorbed Mrs. D.'s perspective on classroom accidents;

in its retelling, "Larry's accident" was about connection-making: specifically about how the members of this classroom community were linked through shared experience and care to one another and to the broader school-wide community. Re-created was a portrait of the principal, Mrs. N., who, hearing the commotion while passing down the hall, rolled up her sleeves and got right in there with paper towels. Next the irascible head custodian was called in, and, having quickly sized up the required clean-up operation, supplied Larry with a body-size garbage bag, cut a head-size whole cut in the center of the bottom, and slipped it over Larry's head so he could get out of his paint-soaked clothing "in privacy." The art teacher, Mrs. Mott, being the only teacher with access to a large sink, was consulted by phone in her room. She agreed to wash Larry's clothes herself. Later the class observed her hanging them on a tree out on the school's front lawn to dry.

Eventually, this story for the classroom chronicle was completed during yesterday's writing workshop by Larry and Mrs. D. working with a small group of volunteers while the other children pursued their ongoing writing. But not before the "lessons" of the whole-group narration had been summarized by Mrs. D. for application to the children's individual work: "Use the speaker's exact words. Show us the evidence!"

Vignette #11: "Seeing things from different perspectives"

Today Mrs. D. begins the mini-lesson by invoking a character out of her own life story who is very familiar to the children. Mrs. D.'s very old Aunt Vy, a woman quite dependent on Mrs. D. despite her bluster to the contrary, frequently finds her way into this classroom by way of humorous stories. The stories typically focus on some aspect of the conversation during their regular Sunday afternoon outings. The children know that Aunt Vy is hugely entertained by the stories from their own classroom that Mrs. D. brings her.

The entire class is intently focused on the whiteboard at the front of the classroom as Mrs. D. writes the following:

Sunday, Aunt Violet didn't think the story about Larry and the paint jar accident was funny. She was angry at me!
"Why [are you angry at me]?" I asked her.
"Well, Judith, you shouldn't have put the paint can near the children."

The children are predictably delighted. That Aunt Vy! Always giving Mrs. D. trouble!

Discussion: Maternal storytelling and the nurturance of teachers

The story provides a fine example of the modeling of the tension between "hav[ing] a life very much [one's] own" and being "inextricably connected with others" accomplished, contends Sara Ruddick, by good maternal storytelling. But now, in front of the children, the lesson is applied to an important adult authority figure in their lives. The children know from the stories she regularly tells them that Mrs. D. loves and cares for Aunt Vy. Yet Aunt Vy clearly drives Mrs. D. crazy. Mrs. D. also values many things about Aunt Vy, including the fact of their relatedness. Mrs. D.'s commitment to Aunt Vy is an important moral one. But Mrs. D. is a moral person who requires moral commitments.

Today Mrs. D. has drawn Aunt Vy into the classroom community as a potential ally for Larry, helping her (Mrs. D.) teach him about other possible perspectives on himself and on adult authority. There is somebody looking out for him even outside the safe haven of this classroom. From Aunt Vy's perspective, Mrs. D. is the culprit, the irresponsible adult who gets a little kid in trouble. There is certainly no "bad boy" in Aunt Vy's version of the story.

But Aunt Vy is also an important resource for Mrs. D. as a subjective being, outside of her complex maternal storytelling role in this community. In Mrs. D.'s "life very much [her] own" Aunt Vy is a valuable ally to her storyteller-self and her writer-self. She is funny, and the telling of her stories makes Mrs. D. funny. These realities intimate the potential for nurturance of the teacher herself in a classroom like this one. Such nurturance is a particularly important consideration when the teachers like the ones on this team are taking on as the point of their work the difficult challenge of fostering an appreciation of their positive connections with others for the children in their care.

Conclusion

By requiring teachers to develop a community of artists in our classrooms, the arts-based social reconstructionist curriculum provides us an opportunity to attend to the educative place of community and/or communal connections in all of our lives. Related, it also provides a model for creating a community in which the world is re-shaped in microcosm. Finally, teachers have the opportunity to grow in our capacity to artfully shape the life in the classroom, while simultaneously challenging ourselves to expand the boundaries of our own lives. Such an opportunity offers another take on the parallel practices theme: the elementary teacher's personal growth and her classroom's curriculum.

The next chapter further develops the theme of the teacher's personal growth, linking that growth to a commitment to community activism as an extension of the teacher's work in her own classroom. In this case, I am the teacher, and I explore my own work and potential work in the teacher education classroom. But an analogy is suggested that creates a further connection between these two chapters: the parallel relationship of "practice for . . ." and "the real thing" to literacy assignments that remain in school versus literacy assignments that travel out into the community.

Chapter Four
Using Multicultural Literacy Assignments to Inspire Social Action as Curriculum: *Salman Rushdie's* Haroun and the Sea of Stories *Illuminates My (A Teacher Educator's) Community's Development Crisis*

Assignment

If Cassie Louise Lightfoot from Faith Ringgold's *Tar Beach* (1991) brought into her public school classroom her dreams of flight and racial equality, including her hopes that her Dad will find the secure honorable work he deserves and that her Mom could know some ease, and Cassie's teacher was Codi Noline from Barbara Kingsolver's *Animal Dreams* (1990), what kinds of experiential learning, student writing, and local activism might be generated there? What books and articles might the students read to propel this curriculum? Which community members might the students want to interview and what questions might they generate to ask the interviewees? You will need to make adjustments in historical era, subject specialization, age range of students, and geographical regions. Allow those adjustments to affect the social construction of the characters. Also assume that this teacher modeled on Codi Noline had undertaken the same very focused study of John Dewey's *The School and Society The Child and the Curriculum* (1902/1990) that you have recently undertaken in this program. Keep in mind Dewey's assumption that children want to use their imaginations to tackle real obstacles in the world.

Assignment

The sister and older daughter Lia in Ann Fadiman's ethnography *The Spirit Catches You and You Fall Down* (1997) is assigned an autobiographical essay shortly after beginning her new school in California. She writes about her (Hmong) family's grueling journey to Thailand in escape from Laos (after the U.S. reneged on a promise of protecting the Hmong people it used to fight its own war) including the experience of near starvation, her witnessing the murder of extended family members, and the death of a younger sibling. Her teacher writes in response to her essay, "You have had an exciting life." We have already established in class that the teacher's response, though probably well intentioned, was likely hurtful to Lia. Now pretend that Lia had a teacher who had given much thought to the intertwined issues of the global economy, race, and war as a result both of her having sought out a critical multicultural education and her efforts to come to terms with her own social positioning. Perhaps it would be helpful to model this fantasy teacher on Ntozake Shange's character, Betsey Brown; she'd need to be older, re-situated in the current historical era, and have made the decision to become a teacher! What might she have written in response to Lia's essay? Being respectful of the obvious need for sensitivity to Lia's right to control information about her own life, can you imagine a possible range of invitations to curricular collaboration she might have extended to Lia?

The relationship between these fantasy assignments and my own work in teacher education

At SUNY Binghamton we are continually revising the curriculum of our social justice–focused master's program in elementary education. At the heart of the program is a conception of *social action as curriculum*; that conception has led to the development of a course of that name, and that course has become increasingly integrative of the program's goals. During my second experience teaching it, my students deepened our connections with a particular local community, historically a refugee resettlement area, through a second public cultural histories mural project, this time at an elementary school. Social contradictions related to issues of multicultural equity-oriented teaching became concrete to some of my students for the first time. And I faced the reality that my own fairly proficient grasp of critical theory and feminist post-structuralism did not help me decide what we should do when social contradictions expressed themselves concretely and required "an answer."

For instance, how could I explain to a beloved principal that my students would need to paint *out* the American flag that had been previously painted *on* the side of the school building featured in the mural at that principal's request? We had agreed with international peace mural policy that because our goal was to help children envision a world without (arbitrary) national borders, we would ban flags from the mural. Puerto Rican children, Kurdish children, and Somali children had conformed to this rule after we explained the rationale to them. To feature an American flag would be unthinkable. It turned out that the PTA felt otherwise. And some of my students had hopes of getting teaching positions in this school after graduation! (We *did* paint over the flag, and we did maintain our positive relationship with the principal. But two PTA officers boycotted our mural "opening.")

I am convinced that we need expanded resources of Deweyan imagination in order to face the challenge of *teaching against the grain*[1] and also promoting a vision of teacher social activism. For we must accomplish these lofty but necessary goals while appropriately protecting our students and offering the concrete skills in curriculum development and classroom management that our students also need. Imaginative literature, memoir, and ethnography exist because people believe that there is something valuable, even transcendent in the sharing of the struggles and tentative resolutions of one another's lives. Why not use these artforms for the real guidance they might offer to our quest for expanded imaginative resources?

The specific course Social Action as Curriculum has offered me the opportunity to experiment with strategic combinations of text to motivate community activism while reinforcing the combined goals and rationale of what we now teach separately as curriculum, social studies, multiculturalism, and children's literature. At this point I have enacted enough imagination to set a limited number of texts in conversation with one another. (See Chapter 5.) But the critical work with text has largely remained in the classroom.

In this chapter I am playing with some of my own emergent understandings about how the use of imaginative multicultural literature, memoir, and ethnography might empower social justice–focused activism *as curriculum* outside of the teacher education and the elementary school classroom. I am thinking about this use of what I've been calling *life-text*, for parallel practice implications beyond my usual concern for modeling with our teacher education students what we want them to be doing with children.

I am reporting here on my own "trying out" of an assignment similar to the two that introduced this chapter in order to suggest how we as social justice–focused teacher educators might do our work more imaginatively in the Deweyan sense. Specifically, I think we might begin to reshape the terrain of own work by bringing some of what has proven inspiring in our classrooms at the university out into the world outside of the classroom. I am talking about the possibility of spiraling our social justice–focused curriculum into the community, thereby making it part of the *curriculum* of the community's life.

The inspiration for such an experiment, the experiment reported on in this chapter, emerged from a real encounter with a work of art similar to encounters with art I have tried to build into my courses. I was serendipitously positioned in this encounter so that I could imagine a conversation between this work of art and the life of my community that was particularly intriguing to me, given my belief in the reality of the *dialectic of freedom*. I was able to put aside all cynicism and re-remember my own belief in political and spiritual resources yet to surface.

The experience began with my eleven-year-old daughter's

insistence that we attend as a family, and support her in testifying at, the hearings about the commercial development plans for the southwest area of the city in which we live, Ithaca, New York. The hearings were announced at morning meeting in her public combined middle school–high school, the Alternative Community School, which is a participant in the Coalition of Essential Schools. It so happened that during the same week my thirteen-year-old son played storyteller Rashid Khalifa in his middle school's production of a dramatic adaptation of Salman Rushdie's young people's novel, *Haroun and the Sea of Stories.*

The hearings, demanded of the city by grassroots activists in an organization called the Citizen's Planning Alliance were held first and included so compelling an invitation to local activism around the issues of economic democracy at the heart of my work and thought that I was already planning attendance at the next CPA meeting. But it was the way the Rushdie play spoke to this cause at this moment that awakened my determination to find my own place, a social justice–focused teacher educator's place, in the opposition campaign against the city's current process and plans regarding what is known as "big box" type (high-volume discount stores typically housed in box-shaped buildings) commercial development.

So when I was asked by the editor of *Bookpress*, Ithaca's free monthly Newspaper of the Literary Arts published by a downtown independent bookstore and distributed in diners, cafés, bagel shops, community centers, supermarkets, and the local universities, to write about the issues raised at the hearings, I saw a special invitation to try out a fantasy assignment, one I might be able to use in Social Action as Curriculum.

Assignment

Working with your small group, use the dramatic adaptation by Tim Supple and David Tushingham of Salman Rushdie's *Haroun and the Sea of Stories* (1999) that we have studied in our course or an appropriate selection of farcical imaginative literature of your choice to illuminate any local issue/cause related to power, privilege, and/or our program's commitment to the pursuit of economic and social democracy including environmentalism as a necessary foundation for quality public education. Investigate with your small group local advocacy organizations and alternative newspapers as well as the mainstream press and other literature in order to locate a viable cause. Interview advocates and opponents and collect as much available literature as you can before beginning the writing. Allow the play to speak to your cause, including appropriate citations from both the play and the data/literature about the cause which you collect. Shape your writing for the appropriate local newsletter, journal, or college paper that might publish it. Or, do all of the above in a videotape and make arrangements to show it at a community center or other appropriate public place.

Rationale for the assignment

The assignment is intended to address the building of that emergent post-structuralist political movement intimated by Maxine Greene that has lost the illusion of shaping a universally shared consciousness, but substitutes a coalition composed of Clifford Geertz's "disorderly crowd of not wholly commensurable visions." (Greene, 1995, p. 185). My graduate students in elementary education are positioned by the assignment itself to become members of this "disorderly crowd." Indeed, one could argue that to require of graduate students that they adopt and enact a social vision necessarily "disorders" conventional graduate student identity, making it possible for individual students to try on new, multiple, and possibly more expansive subjectivities that will possibly enliven the "crowd."

Yet in enacting the assignment, they operate as a collectivity participating in the building of such a movement; they are addressing issues of economic democracy and social justice while strategically reaching out to teachers by joining with them in their quest to enliven literature for *their* students. They raise the possibility that the use of multicultural imaginative literature to make sense of life could become more than a school exercise, instead, a way to promote dialogue through shared experience with text, on issues about which we might disagree.

With this use of literature modeled in the culture, children, who begin school with delight about both oral and written language and what it can do, might retain that delight because they see the potential for strategic use of language to reinvent community life. The possibility emerges of building a new and more flexible regionally influenced canon, one that could include the text that gets generated in response to differently constructed students and teachers facing new social and political challenges in their own communities.

Another rationale for the modeling of this assignment in *Bookpress* has to do with Rushdie's contradiction of the popular assumption, certainly initially held by most of my teacher education students, that the mood of social critique and activism is necessarily heavy. Certainly this assumption is shared by the majority of my students until we successfully contradict it through our work together. Salman Rushdie shares with other writers of the most compelling multicultural fiction an unwillingness to collude with the politics of internalized oppression. Having survived the *fatwah* issued against him driving him into a life underground, Rushdie has maintained a broad and humane perspective on issues of privilege, power, and domination. While recognizing both evil and domination, he parodies the easy construction of goodies and baddies, reminding us continually of the fear of death we all share along with the challenge to resist the attraction (generated by this fear) to either orthodoxies or excessive power. This richness of perspective, the blending of the psychological, spiritual, and political, typical of the multicultural imaginative fiction I have already used in classes, resonates with our education students and teachers, some of whom resist critical and feminist post-structuralist theory for reasons other than its syntactic inaccessibility and their defensiveness around their own privilege.

Many of our students are attracted to education out of one certainty: their basic fascination with people. They love collecting stories about the uncanny understandings of the children they teach, about the rigidities they witness in the hallways and the teachers' rooms, about the funny things that happen during a typical day. Often realistically appreciating the complex limitations and strengths of themselves and others from a richer psychological than political perspective, they cannot resonate with a flattened portrait of human beings as thoroughly identified with their political and economic interests. Rushdie can't either. His humor plays to adolescents and to the perpetual adolescent in all of us. You can tell he thinks if he had too much power, he'd be in trouble too! The bottom line for him is our spiritual interconnectedness, even with our enemies; we are all Mr. Butts (see below) some of the time.

And on that note . . .

I do my own assignment and it gets printed in *Bookpress*

The City of Ithaca has proposed a plan to develop in the district known as the Southwest, one million square feet of retail space of the big chain discount store variety in order to generate sales tax as a source of much needed revenue. At the hearings, speakers focused on a multiplicity of troubling issues related to the city's pursuit of big box development, some regarding the likely impact of this development on both the future vitality of downtown and on wages for the lowest-paid workers locally, some on a complex of environmental issues, many on how these stores exploit both undervalued resources and people of color in developing countries and many on the city's highhanded and possibly illegal tactics, including the overturning of a fill permit denial to the developer, issued by a building commissioner who later was fired. A frequent theme among those who spoke at the hearings, the overwhelming majority of whom were opposed to the plan, was the ethically questionable nature of the city attorney's ruling overturning that fill permit denial, permitting the city to segment the environmental review process in such a way as to make possible the dumping of 80,000 cubic yards of gravel fill by this same developer, at a critical flood-plain site across from Buttermilk Falls State Park.

The play based on Rushdie's novel is about politics, too; its ultimate message, get control over people's stories and you can control the world; let the story stream flow freely and no single force can dominate. To save our stories from being poisoned or plugged up is related to recognizing the insanity of armies (in the play the good guys win the war because they have no discipline), rejecting all orthodoxies, and questioning long and hard whether science/technology/consumer goods really can manufacture happy endings.

The play begins with a classical chorus that resonates with the fears for our city's future voiced at the hearings:

> Chorus: There was once, in the country of Alifbay, a sad city, the saddest of cities, a city so ruinously sad that it had forgotten its name. In the north of the sad city stood mighty factories in which (so I'm told) sadness was actually manufactured, packaged and sent all over the world, which never seemed to get enough of it. Black smoke poured out of the chimneys of the sadness factories and hung over the city like bad news.
>
> And in the depths of the city, beyond an old zone of ruined buildings that looked like broken hearts, there lived a happy young fellow by the name of Haroun, the only child of the storyteller Rashid Khalifa . . . (p. 1)

The action progresses quickly from this ominous beginning, with the unbearable sadness of the city predictably contaminating the lives of the storyteller and his family. The beloved Soraya, Rashid the storyteller's wife and Haroun's mother, abandons them, running off with the upstairs neighbor, Mr. Sengupta. Soraya leaves Rashid the following note, which he reads aloud:

> You are only interested in pleasure, but a proper man would know that life is a serious business. Your brain is full of make-believe, so there is no room in it for facts. Mr. Sengupta has no imagination at all. This is OK by me. Tell Haroun I love him, but I can't help it, I have to do this now. (p. 5)

The identification of "an old zone of ruined buildings" with Ithaca's downtown was instantaneous for me, especially later in the play when Iff the Water Genie laments its probable fate:

> Iff: The Old Zone is where the Source of Stories is located, from which the ancient stories flow. You know how people are—they want new things, always new. The old tales, nobody cares. But if the Source itself is poisoned, what will happen to the Ocean—to us all? (p. 33)

It is Soraya's note, however, that triggers my self-conscious awareness about participating in an important conversation with art. *This woman leaves her beloved husband and child; that's how desperate she is for lack of imagination.* And I recognize the play on words as the sentence forms in my mind. She is desperate because of her lack of imagination; she is in desperate pursuit of a lack of imagination.

As a teacher educator I find my students continually inspired by John Dewey's understanding of human imagination. He contradicted the sentimentalized conception of the child's imagination as focused on the unreal and the asocial, viewing that conception as both symptom and cause of his era's love affair with behaviorism. He observed, rather, the desire of children both to make sense of their social reality by imagining, and to participate in their community as the project of the use of imagination toward their own growth. His model of community was an interdependent democracy and the famous labschool he designed had children learning through what he called *occupations*, actually the hands-on study of the doing and making historically required to sustain human communities.

For Dewey, the division of labor between cultured people and workers was antithetical to the nature of human beings, 99 percent of whom were not distinctly intellectual, but rather wanted to use their imaginations to design a work and social life, including an aesthetic life, that made sense in the context of living in a democratic community. (Developers avoiding dialogue with the community had no place in the Deweyan vision.)

Soroya has lost all touch with her own imagination in this sad,

sad town where production has no relationship to what people need and even her husband's storytelling is, we assume, increasingly disconnected from any real audience. The note she leaves captures for me the peculiar wild emptiness of our city's pursuit of big box retail. Here is the same abandonment of precious *family*: sensitive wetlands and the majestic views from Buttermilk Falls already compromised by 80,000 cubic yards of gravel fill on a illegally segmented portion of the Southwest development parcel. This in the name of *urgent need for development* despite the universally acknowledged failure of the model in the current historical era!

The play responds with an appropriate perspective on both *need* and *urgency*: Rashid and Haroun leave their city, which is now *too weepy for words*, and travel into the surrounding letter-named countryside, where Rashid will tell made-up stories whose unabashed integrity will help elect local politicians:

> Chorus: It was almost election time. And it was well known that nobody ever believed anything a politico said. But everyone had complete faith in Rashid because he always admitted everything he told them was completely untrue. So the politicos needed Rashid to help them win the people's votes. (p. 6)

In his sorrow over the loss of his wife, nothing but barks come out of Rashid's mouth in the Town of G. He is threatened with dismemberment by angry politicos, and accompanied by his protective son Haroun, he flees on a speeding bus to the Valley of K, where he promises a "terrifico" performance. It turns out the bus driver, Mr. Butt, is a philosopher of sorts:

> Rashid: Do we need to go so blinking fast?
> Mr. Butt (the busdriver): Need to stop? Need to go so quickly? Well, Need's a slippery snake, that's what it is. The boy here says that you, sir, Need a View Before Sunset, and maybe it's so and maybe no. And some might say that the boy here Needs a Mother, and maybe it's so and maybe no. And it's been said of me that Butt Needs Speed, but but but it may be that my heart truly needs a Different Sort Of Thrill. Oh, Need's a funny fish: it makes people untruthful. (p. 11)

During election season here in Ithaca, local politicians are quick
to present themselves as Mother to Ithaca's unique character (often
including its View Before Sunset, not to mention its vibrant downtown arts community, held together with a web of independent
bookstores), but the definition of that character is quite conveniently
a funny fish; it changes when anybody calls for its preservation.
(Need to stop?) And what will the city sell to developers at what
Speed? Now a former Common Council member tells us that there
was no discussion of an earlier higher bid on land recently sold to a
developer negotiating with Borders. (Need to go so quickly?) And
the contorted language of the purchase agreement reveals the city's
effort to cover up probable environmental contamination of the site.

> Mr. Butt: It was a figure of speech. But but but I will stand by it! A figure
> of speech is a shifty thing: it can be twisted or it can be straight. (p. 9)

The bus ride continues, and Haroun convinces Mr. Butt to stop
for a view of the sun setting over the Valley of K, a view Rashid has
often described to his son as incompatible with sadness. Indeed,
the view has that effect on Rashid:

> Rashid: Thanks, son. For some time I thought we were all done for, finito,
> Khattam-shud.
> Haroun: Khattam-Shud. Wasn't that a story . . . ?
> Rashid: Khattam-Shud is the Arch-Enemy of all Stories, even of Language
> itself. He is the Prince of Silence and the Foe of Speech. And because
> everything ends, because dreams end, stories end, life ends, at the finish
> of everything we use his name. 'It's finished,' we tell each other, 'it's
> over. Khattam-Shud: The End.' (p. 13)

There's a dialectical relationship between hope and storytelling
modeled here, and some useful information about human resilience
that teachers, in particular, might appreciate. Rashid the storyteller
has remained cheerful despite the sadness that has descended on
his town, causing it to lose its name; there is certainly some sugges-
tion of denial on his part. The factories spewing smoke have

apparently poisoned everything, but Rashid, magically connected to the Story Waters in the Great Story Sea, loses his hope only when his beloved wife, his deepest and most intimate connection to humanity, abandons him. Only then is the message of his own despair in the form of a histrionic soliloquy conveyed by P2C2E (a process too complicated to explain) to Iff the Water Genie, who is at that point obligated to disconnect Rashid from his source of Story Waters in the Great Story Sea. But a View Before Sunset is sufficient inspiration to reverse Rashid's complete desperation.

People who argued at the hearings and continue to argue daily for an understanding of what big box development means from a global/ecological perspective are labeled "elitist" and/or "classist" and/or "non-substantive." The implications are that awareness of our spiritual and economic connections with all others, and with all natural resources, the reality that John Dewey conceived of as the basis for the functioning of human imagination, and Rushdie, the basis for storytelling, is an unfairly privileged state that leads to irrelevant knowledge. In other words, our mayor tells us that you have to be rich to know that you don't deserve a better quality of life purchased at the expense of your neighbor's across town or across the world or through the loss of irreplaceable natural resources.

At the same time, because the real conversation is about making the deal go through, you are not real and your knowledge not substantive when you don't respond to the specifics of the actual development plan. Here you can have real input, the city tells us. What should we require of these corporations, even though they are a more powerful version of the ones we already have that won't pay for traffic lights, even as they threaten to go elsewhere during the very planning process? Loss of Deweyan imagination leads to magical thinking, but not the inspiring kind we find in stories. Instead, we are asked to negotiate with Khattam-Shud.

The problem is that the charge of "elitism," so effective in silencing the dialogue that needs to happen about development issues, works for two reasons: The first is that in an era where the rich are getting richer and the poor are getting poorer at an alarming rate, those of us who live in relative comfort are ashamed and confused. Understanding vaguely that in this new global economy our standard of living is artificially bolstered by the poverty of others, usually of color, often far away, and usually having stories either poisoned or silenced by the Khattam-Shuds of this world, we are perpetually guilty.

The second is that there is some truth to this charge, both within the context of the local debates and in terms of a critique of Progressive era theoreticians like Dewey. John Dewey correctly saw that the division of labor into cultured people and workers was antithetical to the nature of human beings. But what we've learned since Dewey's time is how much of what we call human is open to social construction and destruction. Those who have been able to hold on to or recover the awareness of connectedness to others and to nature, the basis for imagination in the Deweyan sense, and for generating stories in the Rushdie sense, have somehow outwitted the division of labor in our own lives. But we have not successfully fought the global political struggle to end its economic and spiritual domination of the majority.

Sometimes this personal outwitting is accomplished through a process of spiritual awareness and transformation and sometimes it is achieved through education, often "elite" education or the public alternative kind in short supply that you need to be specially positioned to find. (Such is the education we try to provide our teacher education students in our very small program at SUNY Binghamton; such is the education my children get at the Alternative Community School, which always has a huge waiting list.) Using these spiritual or educational resources well typically involves a certain amount of sweat and personal sacrifice, but the sacrifice is usually experienced as a choice. Sometimes the personal process represents a reversal of the patterns of oppressing others and patterns of exploiting the natural world to which one has been socialized; sometimes it represents a reversal of patterns of accepting oppression. Typically it is partial and unfinished, like all human processes, meaning that people are still influenced by past limitations and ongoing disconnections for all of their best intentions of moving toward some conception of a common good. Economic privilege and/or luck often makes such personal transformative processes, incomplete as they are, possible. The point is that without a massive political movement, such transformation is available to the few.

Arts communities, alternative education communities including the social justice–focused teacher education program in which I work at SUNY Binghamton, and ironically, even the kind of inspiring and well-informed protest communities represented at the hearings in Ithaca typically survive in this contradictory space where partial transformations have been achieved by the thinkers, speakers, authors, creators, and performers. The hearings were announced at morning meeting in my daughter's Alternative Community School, precisely because the teachers and administrators there have undergone such transformations. But the survival of such communities is currently dependent on patrons that include many who have simply occupied the privileged pole of the division of labor without angst and with a fully entitled perspective on their own power to direct the workers/students and, in the Rushdie sense, silence a multiplicity of stories.

There are no easy solutions to these contradictions, but again, *Haroun and the Sea of Stories* offers hope. Strategizing about how to defeat Khattam-Shud and his Warriors of Chup, Rashid translates the ancient sign language revived in this silenced community from a renegade officer:

> Don't think all Chupwalas follow Khattam-Shud. . . . Mostly they are simply terrified. (p. 47)

Strategizing on this basis, the war is won, the Sea of Stories is unplugged, and the fortress of Khattam-Shud, including its story-poisoning apparatus, is melted, quite literally, by light, thanks to the son, Haroun. Soraya's love affair with lack of imagination is predictably short-lived, and we are left with the impression that under the influence of Haroun, Rashid has grown out of his earlier self-absorbed befuddlement to become a storyteller with a better capacity to attend to immediate reality.

Though we know that reality is often stranger and more complex than the best of the arts, like this marvelous play produced by the local Montessori Middle School, perhaps we can learn lessons from Rushdie. Perhaps Ithaca's arts, protest, and alternative school communities might unite to develop strategies to address the fears that polarize our city by silencing dialogue and giving power to Khattam-Shud. Perhaps part of this strategizing could be some means of collecting and disseminating the currently silenced stories in our midst. In teacher education, this could mean a more activist use of the equity oriented multicultural fiction available for both adults and young people.

As this book is going to press ethical violations continue to plague the city's negotiations with the developer over the building of big box stores well within the viewshed of our precious Buttermilk Falls. The opposition of local environmental, fair wage, and clean government activists, including the Citizens' Planning Alliance Southwest Committee, of which I am an active member, continues.

At the same time, in this past year my colleagues and myself used an enormous amount of valuable time on the process of re-accrediting our own teacher education program for the bureaucratic "big box" that the State Department of Education increasingly appears to be, while we observed well-intentioned public school teachers give over stimulating and appropriate curriculum to high-stakes test preparation. Progressive teacher educators are joining with parents and teachers in antitesting movement-building to protect the environment of our communities, the communities of social justice–focused teacher education, and public schools.

So it's important to remember that our story is in process. And Rushdie's character, Walrus, synthesizer of Happy Endings by P2C2E, and Haroun leave us with a final bit of wisdom:

> Walrus: Happy endings must come at the end of something. If they happen in the middle of the story, or an adventure, all they do is cheer us up for a while.
> Haroun: That'll do. (p. 74)

The use of such an assignment in a teacher education seminar like Social Action as Curriculum raises many questions related to the parameters of social justice–focused teacher education. An obvious potential problem is that although passionate teacher educators like myself say that we welcome collaboration with Geertz's "disorderly crowd of not wholly commensurable visions," we clearly hope that the crowd will accept *our* vision. There are certainly many controversial issues here relative to the potential for substituting corporate/ state educational bureaucratic control over teacher education curriculum with equally dogmatic, though at this point, significantly marginalized personal agendas. But wouldn't it be great to generate new imaginative literature and theater in which we debate these issues with the teachers, children, and families in our communities!

Postscript

A slightly modified version of my experiment with this assignment appeared in the March 2000 *Bookpress*. It was the most gratifying publishing experience I have ever had. Students, teachers, and parents in the local schools, including, but not limited to, the two my children attend, have responded enthusiastically to me about the piece. People present at the hearings have stopped me on the street to thank me for writing it. Three of my teacher education students at Binghamton University sent appreciative e-mails about it. (I was on a research leave, and was not teaching at the time the article was published.) A well-loved English/Drama teacher at the Alternative Community School is considering the dramatic adaptation of *Haroun* for production at ACS. Another local English teacher asked how to locate a copy of the script. A colleague of mine used in her doctoral qualitative research seminar a follow-up article I wrote about unethical marketing of commercial development for a later *Bookpress*. At the same time, parents and teachers in both Ithaca and Binghamton are beginning to organize "testing parties" designed to build an opposition movement to high-stakes testing. I'm definitely cheered up enough to continue the struggles!

My doing this assignment in the local paper described above is a way of publicly redefining the work of teacher education. If social justice–focused teacher educators see the building of a new political movement as necessary to the continued existence of quality public education, perhaps we need to transfer some of our work energy into helping to build one. Scholarly journal articles continue to have very limited audiences, and their influence on teacher education programs and then, schools, is compromised by the multiple competitive contexts in which they function. More important, writing for the local press puts us in immediate dialectical interaction with other activists who are our potential allies.

My own experience confirms this reality. Attending a Citizens' Planning Alliance meeting while doing the necessary research for my *Bookpress* article, I was introduced to a local solar energy activist, Steve Nicholson. Steve was eliciting the CPA's support for a plan to equip the roof of the currently under construction new Tompkins County Library in downtown Ithaca with photovoltaic solar panels. By contacting the chair of the County Board of Representatives and my own geographic area's representative on the board, I learned that with the vote on this million-dollar solar paneling project only two weeks away, the board was about evenly divided. It was the opinion of both the chairperson and my representative that the vote could actually be influenced by the testimony of a few well-informed young people about the importance of this project. Having already contacted teachers in my daughter's school to follow up on the hearings which had been advertised at a morning meeting, and then discovering that an Eco-Action Committee already existed, I quickly had the support of two teachers and an assistant teacher to organize a presentation by Steve Nicholson for students during this committee's meeting time.

As this book goes to press, our local Board of Representatives voted to approve solar panels for the downtown library roof. Four students from my daughter's school, the public Alternative Community School, testified eloquently at a Board of Representatives meeting and collected hundreds of signatures in favor of the project at the local farmers' market. In this current historical era the opportunity to involve young people in a winnable progressive political struggle gives new and dynamic meaning to the concept of *the teachable moment*. What could compete in importance with the possibility of helping to reverse the cynicism of young people well educated in ecological crisis but having no reason to believe that the adults with real power will act in more than symbolic ways to preserve their world? It is easy to imagine the dialectical impact of a series of wins in these cases, how the students involved would respond to future opportunities to act on behalf of their community out of their own beliefs and knowledge. Here is Maxine Greene's *dialectic of freedom* in action, as well as the social re-construction of imagination in the Deweyan sense.

The content of this chapter has represented half imagination, half-enacted imagination, perhaps intimating the process of being propelled by Adrienne Rich's "wild patience" that Maxine Greene finds so appropriate for our contemporary work in public education. The next and final chapter restricts itself to that which has already been enacted. Hopefully, readers will find it inspiring of their own Deweyan imaginations, that we might begin to build a *social action as curriculum* for the life of our communities. Then we might see the *dialectic of freedom* operating in both directions, generating parallel practices for public schools and teacher education programs based on what is going on in the communities that circumscribe the schools while we teacher educators also continue to strategize from the teacher education classroom outward.

Chapter Five
EDUC 594: Social Action as Curriculum: *From* Animal Dreams *to the Museum of Social Advocacy as Art*

Organization of this chapter

This chapter begins to explore my own recent development of the course Social Action as Curriculum to support a community activist commitment for pre-professional master's students in elementary education. In this chapter I will offer the rationale for this course and briefly identify some of the activist projects pursued by the students during my first two experiences teaching Social Action as Curriculum. I'll also provide a concrete artifact from my third and most recent experience teaching the course, the visitors' guide to the Museum of Social Advocacy as Art, which will help readers appreciate the connections between the text-based content of the course and the choice of projects pursued by my students. But the primary purpose of the chapter is to share my thinking about the text-based work in class with my students that highlights the parallel practice implications of *social action as curriculum.* In other words, I believe that the dialectical process of working with text to develop my teacher education students' compassion and commitment to community social activist work parallels the process they can pursue with children. In some cases, students have already enacted these parallel practices. This pursuit might guide not only community building efforts in the future elementary classrooms of my students, but also their literacy and social studies curriculum. Such a development could pave the way for actual service learning and community activism on the part of children that emerges from the regular curriculum of their classrooms.

With such goals in mind, I have included in this chapter rationales for the use of the Barbara Kingsolver novel *Animal Dreams* (1990) and the memoir by Barack Obama, *Dreams from My Father* (1995), which should offer enough information that readers could strategize about similar use of comparable texts. Also featured in the chapter are some of the actual lesson plans that I use to develop the themes from *Animal Dreams* which prepare students to select and commit to an activist project. Those same themes also organize the course. I have written less extensively about our work with the Obama text, but include here one study guide and a more integrative assignment specifically focused on racism that I have used with that text. Hopefully, these assignments will suggest to readers the continuity of our text-based work and the escalation of depth in emotional, political/intellectual, and spiritual challenge I try to build into our process. As well, I briefly address the way I integrate critical theoretical text and film into our readings as support for both growth in student consciousness and background information to feed the competence with which projects are pursued. Following this discussion I present a listing of projects students have enacted, a few highlights from mural projects, and the visitors' guide to our Museum of Social Advocacy as Art introduced above, which offers some indication of the content and spirit of our most recent activist work. A brief conclusion summarizes my future hopes for this work.

Rationale for Social Action as Curriculum

The socially critical scholarly literature in our field confirms that our now traditional "progressive" methods of teaching education students how social inequities are perpetuated through public schooling meet with discouraging results as often as otherwise; my own experience confirms that courses based on laissez-faire discussion of critical theory and feminist post-structuralist texts tend to move those students already predisposed to seeing the world from critical intellectual perspectives. As well, the language of radical social analysis based on critique of social class domination and white privilege typically offered by critical theorists and feminist post-structuralists is accessible to only our most education-privileged students; one could argue that the language itself perpetuates privilege by making valuable information inaccessible to the practitioners who might be able to use it to struggle for social justice.

After working in elementary teacher education and closely related fields for many years, I have observed that some of the most inspired elementary teachers who work beautifully with socially diverse groups of children do not successfully read this literature, a reality which would certainly not surprise John Dewey. People who want to explore the world with children, including many who have reasonable intellectual standards for this collaborative pursuit, are not typically the same people who want to dissect and generate critical theory and feminist post-structuralist critique.

It is also the case that in this sometimes socially paralyzing post-structuralist era, with its multiple identities and political locations, we know that the lessons learned by our students through a professor-initiated race, class, and gender critique of prevailing social inequities replicated in schools are extremely variable and unpredictable. I place this uncertainty against the backdrop of what I know: I know that I want my students to become activists, not experts in radical social critique. I want them to use what they begin to understand in order to struggle for a more just social world through their work as teachers. And my experience has taught me that a parallel practices approach to curriculum making for elementary teacher education, where our curriculum with our students replicates what we want them to be doing with children, is an effective way to ensure that our students' emerging vision of curriculum for their own elementary classrooms will be social reconstructionist in its orientation.

Rationale for the use of imaginative
literature and memoir in a social foundations course

Discussion of *The Dialectic of Freedom* in Chapter 2 established the value of using *life-text* generally and of Greene's particular account of the dialectical process of "opposing obstacles" with elementary education students. But carefully selected imaginative literature and memoir can offer more detailed information than the scope of Maxine Greene's book makes possible about how people come to this commitment to "overcoming obstacles." Further, Greene's text is not intended to focus on the *dialectic of freedom* as it has historically engaged classroom teachers; rather, it asks teachers to ally with those who have moved toward greater social justice as writers and participants in a wide range of historical U.S. liberation movements.

Social Action as Curriculum has as its stated goal the movement of my students toward a specific teacher-activist identity. In this course I have found Barbara Kingsolver's fictional *Animal Dreams* and Barack Obama's memoir *Dreams from My Father* to provide excellent preparation for my students' process of enacting a social activist commitment in our community. And interestingly, intimate study of these texts has made carefully selected presentations of critical theory and feminist post-structuralist critique accessible for the first time to many of my students.

I use both the Kingsolver and Obama texts in an unabashedly deterministic way: I design assignments that move my students to identify with aspects of the social construction of the activist characters so that they might learn some of the lessons of the characters' lives. The most significant lesson is a reinforcement of Dewey's equation of "human life" with "mind-body in wholeness of operation," a confirmation that engagement with the *dialectic of freedom*, although a choice, is a human imperative. In the words of Ernest Becker, author of the Pulitzer–prize winning *The Denial of Death*: "Beyond a given point man is not helped by more 'knowing,' but only by living and doing in a partly self-forgetful way. As Goethe put it, we must plunge into experience and then reflect on the meaning of it" (p. 199).

The Kingsolver and Obama books have a great deal in common, in that their powerful central characters voice their own processes of gradual political radicalization through increasing personal self-awareness as people and teachers, continually reinforcing the message so especially useful to the students I teach who have decided to become teachers that *the personal is political.* The Kingsolver text features a new female teacher who is forced to face, among other realities, her own related patterns of fear and entitlement. Her struggles are readily accessible to the majority of my students who are white and female; therefore, I teach *Animal Dreams* first. Issues of race, social class, and economic globalization are certainly prominent in the Kingsolver text, but they are experienced from the perspective of a white middle-class person who is gradually becoming enlightened and most important, acts on what she comes to understand, despite internal resistance. Most helpfully for my purposes, the narrative voice positions main character Codi's resistance to taking action as symptom of the self-damaging psychological patterns which unravel during the course of the novel. In effect Codi (and her sister, Hallie) prepare my students for Barack Obama, whose memoir takes on racism and social class oppression in multiple manifestations, but as in the Kingsolver text, never splits apart the political and the psychological, never marginalizes one in favor of the other. Barack Obama is bi-racial, and grows up in Hawaii with a Midwestern white mother and a mostly absent African father who is a Kenyan government official. Once an adult, Barack Obama, like Codi and Hallie, becomes an activist (not exactly a teacher, but a teaching community organizer), always processing "personal experience" through that activist identity.

Rationale for using
Animal Dreams with teacher education students

Animal Dreams features the return to Grace, Arizona, her childhood home, of Codi Noline, failed (in her own assessment) medical student and twin sister to beloved Hallie, a plant pathologist who has recently left a makeshift living arrangement with her sister to bring her skills to peasants struggling against a U.S. military–backed fascist dictatorship in Nicaragua. Hallie's departure has precipitated Codi's decision to come back to the working-class and multiply mixed-race Grace to offer whatever support he'll accept to their (she and Hallie's) emotionally remote physician father, who apparently is in the early stages of Alzheimer's disease.

Beginning with her decision to sign on as Grace's formally unqualified high school biology teacher, Codi narrates with excruciating self-consciousness what she conceives of as her struggle to belong to this working-class Latino, white, and Native American community as motherless daughter, teacher, partner, friend, sister to the physically absent but emotionally ever-present Hallie, and, until revealed as otherwise, white person of privileged ancestry. The main character's relationship with a mixed-background Pueblo and Apache Native American, Loyd, becomes one of many contexts in which she is forced to confront the feelings of entitlement she has internalized that contribute to her ambivalence about belonging. The novel is constructed so that three parallel processes related to Codi's growth are explored simultaneously: her gradual commitment to the relationship with Loyd, her development into an inspired social reconstructionist biology teacher who involves her students in the community's opposition to the poisoning of its river by a mining company's leaching operation, and the uncovering and reinterpretation of memories from her childhood which propel her commitment to this community.

Although Kingsolver's novels, and particularly her recent epic *The Poisonwood Bible*, have met with critical acclaim, in her earlier writing, which includes *Animal Dreams*, the author is sometimes accused of overdetermining her characters and overmoralizing in the service of a politically left-liberal and New Age spiritually influenced social critique. But I see her efforts as unusually productive for my students' learning, and conceive of her writing as a kind of historically justifiable affirmative action, seeking to draw attention to how complex social, political, and psychological phenomena help define "who we are." I also identify strongly with the complexity of the task she sets for her characters, who, in effect, reintegrate for the reader the personal/ psychological, spiritual and political contexts that have collectively contributed to their (the characters') social construction. This reintegration is critical for my students, some of whom have thought about social construction issues only in relation to individual and/or family systems psychology.

Interestingly, the devaluation of the personal/psychological was supported in the fields of curriculum studies and social/political foundations of education by many well-intentioned progressives I have considered my allies. They quite correctly contested the over-psychologizing of the problems of people, including the problems in our schools and communities, positing that psychologizing social problems served to mask the deeper causes of these problems in political domination and related social and economic inequity. The progressive critique appropriately acknowledged that while we would need to muster political will, and particularly the political will of its short-term beneficiaries to effectively challenge poverty and social malaise rooted in racism, classism, and sexism, problems presented as psychological would invite easy sympathy and the simple personal directive to get help/therapy as opposed to engage in grassroots organizing.

But the close relationship between personal and political ills, articulated as theory perhaps most directly by Albert Memmi (1965) in his analysis of how individual people are psychologically damaged by the internalization of thought and behavior patterns associated with being members of both oppressor and oppressed groups, is particularly important for my students and myself. Most of my students have never been invited to seriously consider the implications for their beliefs and practices as teachers of the more socially and politically complex conception of what Maxine Greene calls "situatedness" referring to the familial, social class, geographic, ethnic, and religious communities of identification in which they and their students have lived their lives.

Though elementary education graduate students are exposed to issues of social construction of knowledge and identity in typical progressive foundations courses, readings in critical theory and feminist post-structuralism tend to marginalize the psychological and spiritual conceptions of how people become who they are, the aspects of social construction that are likely initially to be more accessible to our students. Further, it has been my experience that psychologically oriented critique of a character's choices can be readily expanded into a critique of the political and economic forces that helped construct those choices—the very choices that initially appear to be only personal and psychological. In effect, when we look at psychological dynamics of characters who act with good intentions in a quality story that clearly includes a multicultural community scenario, we give our students, without jargon or a level of theoretical complexity that frustrates some of them, the kind of intimate information about how the dynamics of internalized oppression (including self-hate) and internalized oppressor patterns (including class/race privilege and feelings of entitlement) can be reversed in the lives of people with whom they are inclined to identify.

At least as significant, our students are reminded by these well-intentioned characters of the reality of human limitation, a reality not at all foreign to classroom teachers, but notably absent from critical theory and even feminist post-structuralist analysis, both of which tend to make economically driven political and social oppressions responsible for everything wrong with the world, including its schools. The corollary of such a premise is that a successful political struggle to end oppression will solve all the world's problems.

However, students do not see the people making these arguments devoting the primary resources of their lives to the organization of such a political struggle. The product of this contradiction is the purveying of cynicism that Dewey described seventy years ago. (See Chapter 1.) There is nothing more devastating to elementary education than teacher cynicism. The belief that there is really nothing they/we collectively have the power to do to challenge big social problems will surely determine that the curriculum will replicate what already is. Further, and equally devastating, cynical teachers will not recognize in each individual child they teach the potential contributions of their unique (Deweyan) imagination/"developing spirit" (Ruddick, 1989) to the work of healing the world.

Another important reality is that teachers are constantly dealing with their own, their colleagues', and their students' limitations as well as strengths. The extent to which these limitations were engendered and/or reinforced by oppressive patterns in the culture does not change the reality that teachers have to deal with them and strategize around them in the here and now. Related is the issue of the internalized oppression of some of our students; those who have themselves been victimized by oppression, including, of course, sexism, and racism, need information about the perils of internalizing feelings of powerlessness and conversely, the personal empowerment that can come with a commitment to social activism. Our students also need to hear explicitly from us that people who chronically feel like victims do not make good teachers.

Equally important, my students continually remind me how underobserved by many self-identified progressives and reformers in education is the nobility of individual teachers who struggle to make humane choices in severely constrained environments. Particularly when student teaching, they are quicker than I am to appreciate the unusual levels of thoughtfulness behind specific efforts of their cooperating teachers, especially relative to children whose families have been severely damaged by the effects of social oppressions. During their classroom internships, my students converse at great length about the complexity of social contradictions in which teachers teach, many of them underestimated in the theory that seems to suggest that not only "correct" but also effective practices will automatically flow from a teacher who has absorbed a progressive political critique of issues of race, class, and gender.

With Kingsolver's help, the theme of human limitation structures my own introductory work with my students on *Animal Dreams*, affirming for them what I believe is a more realistic appreciation of the challenges of being a self-reflective social justice–focused teacher. By way of pulling the reader into her story of the political and spiritual awakening of teacher Codi Noline, Kingsolver begins the book with a kind of baseline metaphoric yet quantitative assessment of the fear and anger that dominate the psyche of Codi's single parent father, Homer Noline, and by implication, shape Codi's own profound ambivalence and self-doubt as a young adult.

Assignment: Assigning students to locate metaphors of loss and alienation in the text

I have long considered the first two pages of *Animal Dreams* a gift to teacher educators like myself in that this small segment of introductory text is loaded with suggestions and images of social disconnection and individual isolation. The two pages speak to Homer Noline's will to unbind the social and emotional ties with Grace's inhabitants of the daughters whose intellects he will, with exasperating intentionality, traditionally educate.

It is easy to make the association in class between Homer's will and my students' own frequently voiced observation of the fragmented nature of the curriculum they experienced as children and now typically observe in elementary school classrooms. In their own experience, as now, meaningful connections between the lives of the children in families and communities outside of school and what goes on in the classroom are the exception rather than the rule. Perhaps as significant, my students have the opportunity to consider the impacts on their own growth of the various typically well-intentioned "Homer Nolines" who contributed to their own socialization. Some students are remarkably open even in class about how their own abilities and disabilities with regard to forging connections with others and with unfamiliar knowledge were shaped.

Here, in *Animal Dreams*, is a father whose obvious love for his daughters is noted by all of my students, even those who find his behavior extremely restimulating of pain in their own lives. But Homer Noline wants to very specifically control what his daughters, Codi and Hallie, will prize as knowledge, and what they will learn to devalue in their own life experiences. Homer is an example, perhaps a bit extreme, of the processes of socialization that myself and my students have personally experienced. For each of us there is a unique journey of unravelling, post-structuralists would say *deconstructing*, the socializing processes that have left us both enabled and disabled to connect with certain kinds of people and not others and to access certain kinds of knowledge and not other kinds.

I want my students to recognize the defense mechanism of "disconnection" as a recurring theme in the wider culture, so that they can develop a critique of their own tendencies to 1) see content area knowledge in discrete categories, 2) to generalize their own very specifically situated social perspectives as universal, and 3) to divorce the operations of mind, heart, and body—thinking, feeling, and acting. The hope is that such awareness will allow them to access for their own curriculum-making the lessons of Dewey's conception "mind-body in wholeness of operation."

Assignment

Trace all images of disconnection in the first two pages of Kingsolver's *Animal Dreams*. Feel free to think metaphorically. Decide in your small group whether you want to work individually and pool your discoveries/findings, or whether you want to brainstorm as a group. As always, select one person to report back to the whole group.

Although the process of small groups responding to this assignment has varied widely, I have consistently observed a kind of self-conscious delight in awakened awareness on the part of some students when others in their group have identified the death or absence of the Noline girls' mother as a separation. A similar response has typically greeted the realization that Homer practices obstetrics, and that the image of delivering a baby is an image of separation. In one experience teaching this course a student in the class who had been a practicing midwife offered the group a fascinating informal presentation about the differences in philosophy between midwifery and obstetrics, articulating, "My practice is less about separation and more about empowering the mother to make intentional contact with the baby, and the baby to make intentional contact with its mother." With input from two other students, she articulated a feminist interpretation of her work, creating an opportunity for me to briefly introduce in our next class both Ruddick's conception of maternal thinking/maternal storytelling and what Eleanor Hartsock has named "feminist standpoint theory" (Ruddick, pp. 131–33).

Some groups have been more deeply philosophical and/or lyrical than others, identifying Homer as afraid of connection as a result of the loss of his wife, and therefore threatened by the connections of his daughters to people who will eventually die. Most groups have expressed some intimation of Homer believing in his own social class and racial superiority over his Latino neighbors. On two occasions a student has corrected or questioned the use of the term "Hispanic" by other students, once engendering a discussion that led to the presentation in our class of an on-campus Latino activist in which he quite movingly narrated to the group his own history of coming to terms with the dominant culture's misrepresentation of his own complex identity.

In this assignment based on these two pages of text some groups have noticed details in the setting, including shadow and light, the framing of doorways, the positioning of the girls in relation to their father. Individual students have conveyed an appreciation for studying literature in this way; a number of times I have experienced a few others agreeing with a student who has voiced the disappointment that she never learned to "think this way" before. As well, I would argue, an awakened aesthetic consciousness has in some cases transferred to the work of my students on their arts-based community activist projects like the cultural histories murals and our most recent museum of social advocacy produced by the students in the course. Most inspiring has been the translation into their own work with children of a delight in exploring metaphor and analyzing "what the author and illustrator are trying to tell us" in any selection of children's literature.

Front-loaded assignments

I characterize the above assignment as *front-loaded*, because I use my authority as teacher to *load into it* an assumption based on background information my students might not have had. Front-loaded assignments scaffold students' thinking by offering them the tools to make connections between what might be for them new ways of looking at text or experience. Such assignments offer the challenge of compiling evidence in support of a proposition that is non-negotiable from the instructor's perspective. Because of my own ideological commitments, which transfer to the course, I am unwilling to use class time to debate whether or not most people are socially isolated from others of different social classes and races, and related, whether racism exists and people of color are oppressed.

Rather, these social realities are front-loaded into an assignment, requiring the students to gather evidence in support of them. Thus the assignment begins with an assumption or a hypothesis based on my own assimilation of socialist, feminist, and non-dogmatic spiritual systems of thinking into my own life experience. I don't ask the students to agree with the assumption, which is often voiced in her/his own words by a protagonist from our current text(s). Most effective is use of students' comments during previous class discussions, always recorded and reproduced with their permission. Then I ask the students to gather evidence in support of the assumption presented, and whenever possible, to explore its implications for teacher education and/or the teaching/learning of children.

Here I act on a belief I have acquired doing this work: that a growth continuum exists whereby the *teacher-as-activist* can develop from the *teacher-as-action-researcher,* who in turn develops from the *student-researcher-of-text.* These phases of development often overlap and are mutually supportive. In my experience the process of using assignments which construct students as researchers of text effectively introduces the teacher-as-researcher identity. This identity then transforms from text-based researcher to elementary classroom-based action researcher to community activist when requirements propel students into a broader social context as preparation for their future work. We, in effect, spiral curriculum from text to the classroom to the community.

Assignment

One of the purposes of this course is to feed a self-conscious quest to figure out how we ourselves have come to know what we know, and how we've come to adopt the viewpoints we hold, or think the way we do. The purpose of this quest is to apply our knowledge about ourselves to the task of figuring out what should be taught in schools and how.

We talked about how "Kingsolver almost beats us over the head" (Amy's words) with the social construction message. *Animal Dreams* argues that we are at least in part socially constructed by the psychological dynamics within our families of origin and the social and political dynamics of the communities in which we are "situated." In the course of constructing ourselves/getting constructed we lose memories that are either too painful to process in the limits of our particular social situation(s) or that are continually contested and contradicted by adults in authority and/or by our peers so that we can no longer believe they were real. *Animal Dreams* suggests that in order to grow in important ways as people who will make a difference in this world, we need to reclaim those memories.

At the beginning of the text Codi presents herself as a lost soul. Gradually, though, the theme of loss and lost knowledge is mitigated by a reclaiming of memories and a growing willingness to commit to her life as a project over which she has significant control. Consider Codi's reclaimings of memory in *Animal Dreams*. Trace this process by finding at least three examples of the reclaiming of memory paralleling a new willingness to take some personal responsibility for her own life and/or the life of her community. Also, what appears to empower/make possible the process of reclaiming the specific memory in each case?

This assignment is front-loaded to convince students that the reclaiming of memories can actually empower appropriate activism, carrying people through the intermediate step of contradicting personal powerlessness so they can access Dewey's "mind-body in wholeness of operation." There is a different than typical interpretation of *the personal is political* here and it has been particularly powerful for my students. In effect, they are being asked to deconstruct the therapeutic influences in Codi's current life with an assumption that what is therapeutic moves people toward "mind-body in wholeness of operation." One hope is that my students gradually internalize the social reconstructionist philosophy of our program as one of the therapeutic influences of their current lives.

Learning from the *life-text* of characters in books

When we offer our students the theory of educators we admire, like I do, for instance, when I teach John Dewey's *The School and Society The Child and The Curriculum*, we provide one kind of learning experience where a theoretician, in the case of my example, Dewey, is set up as an expert in relation to our students. There are many conventionally appreciated strengths to this approach, and clearly it is important to teach the work of people positioned as experts, at least some of the time. Yet we can appreciate from our own life experience that the presence of an "expert" typically sets up certain psychological dynamics that are not always helpful in the teaching/learning transaction. "Experts" are not like us by virtue of being experts and are set up to provoke all of our feelings of unworthiness and "not-smart-enough-ness." Teacher educators are further aware that prospective and practicing elementary school teachers are even more vulnerable to such counterproductive feelings, by virtue of their not having chosen to specialize at one subject in which they would have been assumed to have particular expertise.

By contrast, most of us are happy to learn from people we perceive as our peers, regular folks who have proven themselves to have limitations with which we can identify. The characters in quality fiction and memoir that feature social activist teachers can be positioned by assignments to provide such peerful teaching/learning opportunities lacking in our work with theoretical text. The above provides rationale for the following handout to the students offering a lesson plan for the class meeting that has followed their reading of the first third of *Animal Dreams*:

Assignment

This first chunk of *Animal Dreams* contains a great deal of potentially inspiring incidents and observations for teachers. Choose whatever format you like—oral brainstorming, silent brainstorming, group discussion, or individual written responses—as you work in small groups to address the following questions with a special focus on usefully educating teachers:

1) Codi and her students have taken samples from the river and have found it empty of the protozoans that need to be there. What are the implications of Codi giving her biology students the assignment, "Ask your parents what's going on with this river?" (p. 110)

2) Doc Homer's punishment to Codi for "remembering" being on the ship with the nine Gracela sisters and their peacocks was to make her read the entire *Encyclopaedia Britannica*. What parallels are suggested between Homer's behavior toward Codi and the typical functioning of conventional teachers in relation to children/students? How would you like to change the curriculum to address what you believe to be damaging about both Homer's response to Codi and conventional teaching's response to the child/student's "knowing" and process of coming to know? Conversely, what might be useful about reading the entire *Encyclopaedia Britannica*? (p. 48)

3) Look at the title of the chapter Codi is teaching—Matter, Energy, Organization, and Life. Does this strike you as funny? Why or why not? Do you remember chapters with titles like this in textbooks? How did they disappoint you, surprise you, or inform you? What do you wish you had learned in school that might have been included in a chapter/lesson/curriculum named Matter, Energy, Organization, and Life? (p. 82)

4) Understanding that Homer probably has Alzheimer's disease, what is ironic about this reality for this character (as he has been represented for the reader thus far)? In terms of an approach to life that would suggest that the worst of our pain can still provide inspiration for growth, where might loss or disorganization of memory open windows for a man like Homer?

5) Because of the leaching of copper sulfate into the river, the fruit trees in Grace's river-fed orchards are becoming diseased. The symptom is fruit drop. Why does it matter so much to Loyd or why does it move him so much that Codi knows about fruit drop happening in Grace's orchards? What lessons might a good teacher take away from this reality, the reality that it matters to Loyd that Codi knows?

6) "Maybe it's true what they say, that as long as you're nursing your own pain, whatever it is, you'll turn your back on others in the same boat. You'll want to believe that the fix they're in is their own damn fault." If this assertion is true, what would

be an appropriate curriculum/course of study/assignment/ approach for addressing its reality with aspiring teachers or with any other human beings who wanted to empower other human beings through their work? (pp. 88–89)

7) "We're not exactly couple material, are we? Me and Loyd-with-one-L." "I just can't see myself with a guy that's into cockfighting." How do Codi's comments remind you of teacher-room talk? (p. 115)

8) Codi and her sisters were raised "to be different" than Grace. How did this reality serve them ill? Did it also serve them well in any ways? Lessons for teachers?

Other text used with *Animal Dreams*

Use of the text *The Dialectic of Freedom* to teach social foundations knowledge has already been discussed extensively in Chapter 2. Its particular importance with regard to support for this focused study of *Animal Dreams* is in its conception of both "situatedness" and the movement of a *dialectic of freedom*. I use those terms continually in our work with the Kingsolver text, convinced that "situatedness" conveys both the potential empowerment and constraints inherent in any conception of identity, and that the *dialectic of freedom* maintains a focus on spiritual growth in the movement of my students toward political activism. The *dialectic of freedom* must be intentionally seized, even though its seizure will always have unpredictable consequences. My students are taking risks in the direction of their own growth and the growth of others.

The short films *Zoned for Slavery* and *Mickey Mouse Goes to Haiti*, produced and made available at extremely low cost by the National Labor Committee in New York City, have been particularly useful in connecting the realities of global economic exploitation by multinational corporations to the personal consumption experience of both my students and the characters in the memoirs and imaginative literature we read. This significant focus in class clearly influenced the choice of student projects in the most recent experience of Social

Action as Curriculum which produced the Museum of Social Advocacy as Art.

As well, Jean Anyon's classic "Social Class and School Knowledge" (1981) has been particularly effective at helping my students process their own observations about social class differences in the schools where they have learned, interned, and visited. Because Anyon's broad generalizations hold sometimes and not at others, her article is an invitation to fine-tuned critical inquiry about just what messages are being conveyed by different practices and policies the students are observing, not only in schools, but in the community organizations they are beginning to explore in preparation for commitment to an activist project. The Anyon article has evoked quite dramatic connection-making during in-class discussion between my students' diverse schooling experiences and the parenting practices and educational philosophy of characters in our texts, including Homer Noline in Barbara Kingsolver's *Animal Dreams* (1990).

There is a particular delight in the self-conscious awareness that our discussions, propelled by texts that speak to one another so intriguingly, have depth. In some ways we are in uncharted territory; there are no recipes for correct parenting or teaching practices or for how to use our skills to best advantage in a social activist project. For instance, we face as a group that in different ways both of Homer's children commit themselves to the pursuit of social justice through teaching, our goal for ourselves and the children the students will teach. And many aspects of the Noline girls' education were traditional. Some students suggest that although traditional, Codi and Hallie were pushed by Homer to learn vast quantities of potentially educative information, to become expert in what Delpit (1995) calls "the codes of the culture of power." Others point out that the home of the *abuelita* they borrowed from Codi's friend Emelina was very much a child-centered school in its description, full of purposeful and interesting objects apparently open for exploration. Then, too, the Noline girls had open access to the arroyo and the wildlife it sheltered. There was an absence of some typically middle-class restrictions on access to nature and to the potentially educative stuff of people's lives, material, spiritual, and emotional.

When we viewed Homer's parenting in the context of his desperation to hide his "situatedness" as a "Nolinas," students were
able both to identify specific aspects of the internalized oppression
Homer transferred to his daughters and to understand the roots of
that internalized oppression in his treatment by others just like us,
(myself and my students) trained to accept as natural the corporate
practices portrayed in the National Labor Committee films.

My students are quick to identify "teacher-room talk" as a
dominant culture influence in the construction of Homer's internalized oppression, compellingly captured in his moving appeal
for Codi's understanding:

> We were a bad family. Try to understand. We learned it in school along
> with the multiplication tables and the fact that beasts have no souls. I
> could accept the verdict, or I could prove it wrong. (Kingsolver, p. 287)

Students are typically terrifically moved by Homer's gradual
re-evaluation of the choices he has made as a parent and community member, including his assertion to Codi in the same conversation that he "built [his] castle on the graves of [his] family." For a
teacher educator the question becomes how to construct parallel
self-reflective opportunities for our students without turning class
into a therapeutic support group. Fortunately, Linda Christensen's
Reading, Writing, and Rising Up (2000), published by Rethinking
Schools and intended for diverse middle and high schoolers has
proven an excellent text for modeling intentional curriculum-
building in response to this challenge. Christensen links all student
writing to the study of history, with an eye to the liberation movements on which Greene focuses as well. Christensen's format for
poetry, "I'm From," and for prose poetry, "Write that I . . .," allowed
students to explore as language arts and social studies curriculum
aspects of their own situatedness or the situatedness of characters
in our texts with a focus on how such lessons might transfer to
their own current projects in the community and to their current
and future teaching in diverse classrooms. We were able to consider issues related to the rights of children and their families to

control the information they offer about themselves (as discussed in Chapter 3), in the context of the students' parallel concerns about what they were comfortable sharing in our own classroom.

The same films that helped students appreciate how the economic system's valuing of profit-making for the few could shape the general public's construction of who was worthier than whom in turn evoked the environmentally disastrous policies of the mining company and the equally disastrous fashion trends featured in the Kingsolver text. Both company policy and fashion trends ruined the orchards of the "half-breed Hispanic Indian" parents of the children that Homer's daughter, Codi, taught. Deepening the connections even further, Michael Apple's "Education, Identity and Cheap French Fries" (1996) left students with an expanded and even closer-to-home appreciation of the non-metaphoric global meaning of our own consumption. That article provided a strong transition to the Obama text, in which racism was viewed in the multiple contexts of Barack Obama's life as a black child raised by white people, a "minority" college student, an inner-city community organizer, and an American revisiting his African roots. The patterns of internalized colonization explored conversationally by Obama and his sister matched the economic relations described by Apple in an Indonesian context. Finally, the film *Ethnic Notions* offered the U.S. historical context for all aspects of the racial politics introduced in our texts.

Rationale for studying *Dreams from My Father* in Social Action as Curriculum

Although the activist commitments in which my students are becoming involved by the time we begin studying the Obama text militate against the sometimes paralyzing guilt about their own privilege that is an expected phase in the development of racial and class consciousness, the Obama text has proven a good choice for those students who might become overwhelmed by guilt at this point in the term. Barack Obama is bi-racial and he chooses to not disown the whiteness he claims as part of his own legacy. He also recognizes his privilege as a person who was raised middle class. Obama's rejection of black nationalism is educative in itself, coming from a perspective that my students can appreciate is also radical. Even as a black community organizer in an overwhelmingly black community, Barack Obama must make peace with his own whiteness and his own privilege, as do the majority of my students. Obama's experience of isolation while wrestling with the feelings of not belonging to any community resonates with my students who face sudden discomfort with friends and relatives as their perspectives on social class, race, and their own entitlement begin to shift. It is the middle third of the Obama text that explores from multiple perspectives experiences of social isolation and alienation.

Assignment: Study Guide, second third of Barack Obama's Dreams from My Father

Bring to class your responses to the following questions which will guide our discussion:

1)   Do you agree with Marty that (p. 130) "anger's a requirement for the job. The only reason anybody decides to become an organizer. Well-adjusted people find more relaxing work." Does one need to be angry in order to want to change the world? And what does "well-adjusted" mean anyway?

2)   On p. 136 Harold Washington's mayoral victory is likened to Joe Louis's knockout of Max Schmeling in 1938. There is a reference to this fight in Maya Angelou's *I Know Why the Caged Bird Sings* that really conveys what that victory meant to African Americans. Ask any African American you know over the age of sixty what (s)he remembers about the event or find the reference in Angelou's memoir.

3)   (p. 137) "I tried to imagine what would happen if Gramps walked into the barbershop at that moment, how the talk would

stop, how the spell would be broken; the different assumptions at work." Barack is enjoying feeling accepted for the moment by these black men in the barbershop, including Smitty, "who still burns from a lifetime of insults, of foiled ambitions, of ambitions abandoned before they've been tried," when he imagines his white grandfather entering the shop. Think about and briefly write up a memory of any similar situation in your own life. You were being accepted in part for a marginalized identity and treated like somebody safe to talk to about important feelings but could imagine that "if they only knew" you would not be trusted.

4) On p. 138 Marty is explaining to Barack about the gatherings he'd attended where both blacks and whites, former workers at the old Wisconsin Steel plant spoke of their feelings of shame and betrayal about being unemployed. Why shame? Think about how this feeling of shame about being unemployed gets socially constructed in this society.

5) Read carefully the economic analysis on pp. 168–69. Read the "Cheap French Fries" article. Can you see that the analysis is similar? What is new to you about the perspective offered, if anything?

6) Why does Barack call the stories he is beginning to hear about people's lives "sacred stories"? And why does the recognition that the stories are sacred help him to break out of his own isolation? (pp. 172–75)

7) Pages 176-80 focus on issues of internalized oppression. What are the problems related to dealing with the internalized oppression of specific ethnic, racial, gender, or social class groups in a diverse class, (this course) like ours? How is this difficulty talked about in the text?

8) What is Barack's complex perspective on black nationalism? (pp. 180–88) Why does B. accuse Rafiq of just wanting to change "who got the spoils"?

9) When has rage served you well? When has it served you poorly? If you've never felt rage, how do you feel about never having felt it?

10) I (B. R.) am pretty sure that the play Barack takes Ruby to see (pp. 188–90) is *For Colored Girls Who Have Considered Suicide When the Rainbow Is Enuf* by Ntozake Shange. Please try to see this play at some point in the near future. If you hear of it playing anywhere in the region please let us know. Have you ever seen yourself in a piece of literature or drama in a way that has completely overwhelmed you (in a good way, like it did Ruby)?

11) Does Barack's struggle to make peace with what Auma tells him about his father (p. 203) offer other perspectives on the complex of issues around being "well-adjusted"? And how about the question of anger and the need to struggle for social change? What part might ignorance play in "adjustment"?

12) What is the difference between "real change" (p. 210) and the kind of change Barack appears to believe in at about this point in his life (and experience as an organizer)?

13) On p. 214 the principal, Mrs. Collier, tells Barack that most of these beautiful five- and six-year-old children would lose their laughing eyes, would "shut off something inside" within five years. What kinds of school reform do you think might make it possible for them to not "shut off something inside"?

14) What victory have you ever had that seems to have felt comparable to Barack's small victory as an organizer? (p. 222) Have you ever seen anybody's step do what Sadie's did? (p. 223) "It was as though Sadie's small honest step had broken into a reservoir of hope, allowing people in Altgeld to reclaim a power they had had all along."

15) (pp. 231–32) Let's talk about "good" and "bad" kids!

16) Have you ever been involved on any level in school reform efforts that hit the roadblocks mentioned on p. 234?

17) Let's read aloud Johnnie's story about his dad (p. 238) and discuss the issue of being ashamed of one's parents. Who would like to speak out about their pride in a parent?

18) Referring to pp. 247–48, can we talk about the connections between "social order," hope, hopelessness, and fear?

19) On p. 260, what is the "middleclassness" that Wright's church stands against? And (B. R.'s private question), is there a connection between this quality of "middleclassness" and "well-adjust[ment]"?

20) Referring to p. 262, imagine (plot the course of) "Christian fellowship" between public school administrators and public school parents leading to school reform.

I have found the film *Ethnic Notions* particularly effective after we have finished reading the Obama text. The final integrative assignment links that film to both the Kingsolver and Obama texts and further develops their common themes.

Assignment: Short integrative paper on **Ethnic Notions**

In *Animal Dreams* Codi and the people of Grace encountered a concrete issue of economic oppression when the mining company allowed copper sulfate to leach into the river and the groundwater in order to continue making money from the "tailings" after the mine had closed. The mining company's strategy of diverting the river and, therefore, getting rid of the legal responsibility for the damage, would have left the fruit trees necessary to Grace's livelihood dead and dying. The projected ability of the mining company to "win" against the town was certainly related to the status of Grace's residents as "half-breed Hispanic Indians." Thus we get a clear example of how economic and racial oppression are related.

Barack Obama's life in *Dreams from My Father* illustrates the complexities of racial identity, with Barack constantly dealing with what his race means in different contexts over which he has little control. Further, the meaning of his racial identity shifts even within any single context. Because Barack is well cared for in many ways, his struggle is not always appreciated as important, particularly when assessed by dominant culture readers.

The film *Ethnic Notions* gives us insight into something the people of Grace continually experience and that Barack discovers, that the (white) dominant culture significantly controls the meaning of blackness/color for its own economic/political purposes.

Using specific citations from the texts *Animal Dreams* and *Dreams from My Father* and from the film *Ethnic Notions*, supported by any other knowledge you've acquired in your life including what you've learned in this course, explore how the film *Ethnic Notions* sheds further light on the relationship between the meanings assigned to blackness/color and economic oppression. This is a short paper assignment (5–7 pages average).

Rationale for the preceding assignment

This assignment, too, is *front-loaded*. I have found it helpful to continually restate theoretical understandings that emerge in our course, always modeling the process of theory building in the way I re-access the data from people's lives that my students have already assimilated from our texts. The immediate goal is to help them self-consciously build their own confidence as connected thinkers by offering access to increasingly complex social understandings built from continual invitation to explore the data of diverse people's lives. At the same time, the theory built is immediately reapplied to another related context, bringing self-consciousness to the dialectical process of approaching new resources for learning, in this case, the film *Ethnic Notions*. Again, ultimately the point is to engage in curriculum-making in the teacher education classroom that inspires parallel practices in their work with children and community members both in their projects and in their future classrooms.

The film *Ethnic Notions* has in my experience provoked a

silencing level of guilt among white and dominant-culture students. However, a motivated assignment like this one takes the emphasis off white students' identity as perpetrators or oppressors and puts the emphasis on their potential to educate themselves out of future complicity with the politics of racism, allowing them to challenge an aspect of the conventional politics of whiteness illuminated in both books—not needing to notice—being able to afford not knowing.

This assignment offers a counterweight to the feelings of helplessness and powerlessness the film engenders in different students for different reasons, in part by providing the structure of an intellectually focused viewing experience. By virtue of the assignment, this socially critical film *Ethnic Notions* is positioned differently than is typically the case with films like this one being shown to majority dominant-culture students. The students are researchers of text who will apply their findings to their work in the community. Rather than being set up to provoke defensiveness by informing students of their own historical complicity with racism, the film is positioned by the assignment as in alliance with the teacher-researcher identity our students are required by our program to adopt. As well, its showing is situated in the course to raise a research question that is now accessible to them through our mostly enjoyable process of setting our texts in conversation with one another. And, again, their "findings" in the film will feed student competence in their projects.

The activist projects

In my first two experiences teaching this course my students, typically working in small groups, taught English to local Iraqi activists in the context of working in opposition to the economic sanctions against Iraq, developed a proposal for a local youth credit union, planned and enacted an emergent literacy parent partnership at the Urban League and collaboratively produced three cultural history murals. The first mural project represented a continually negotiated collaboration with one hundred fifty mostly new immigrant

grant Kurdish, Somali, Vietnamese, and Haitian residents of a local housing authority complex. Two other murals involved collaboration with teachers, parents, and children of local diverse urban schools, one an elementary school and one a middle school.

The actual work in the community itself began with the identification of local activists who were motivated by the pursuit of social justice/equity, including, but not limited to, students at Binghamton University. Students and myself worked with them at identifying viable and useful projects that they believed would be compelling to their various constituencies. At that time three years ago we were lucky enough to connect with the local African American activist minister Reverend Henry Ausbey (whose poem is featured in Chapter 3), who had particularly strong ties to some of the new immigrant families living in a housing authority complex near the elementary school in which we have placed approximately one-third of our student teachers. The minister and his wife were interested in creating a public representation of the stories of these families which, in their experience, they were hardly ever encouraged to tell.

Our original project emerged out of the collaboration among this minister and his wife, my students and myself, and the local Arts Council, whose small grant supplied the paints and consulting artist stipends to produce the Saratoga Cultural Histories Mural, named for the housing authority residence whose wall it graces. Over one hundred fifty children and their families worked with us on that mural, including its actual painting. The content of that mural was negotiated at three well-attended public pancake suppers where four translators conveyed the often impassioned words of family members from nine different countries.

Highlights from that project included a spirited evening meeting at the photography studio whose partnership our Bosnian consulting artist had just been invited to join. The meeting included seven female students and a number of local Muslim women and their teenage daughters. At that meeting three Kurdish teenagers and their mothers negotiated with four of my female students and a local Ukrainian artist the plan for the three flying figures that grace the sky at the top of that mural. All representations of teen-age women fleeing oppression, one holds a camera, one a diary, and one, a wedding cake.

During this same project sixty residents filled two buses that took all of us to an informal showing of paintings by the Iraqi artist Ali Makki, completed when he was living in a Saudi refugee camp. A doctoral student in our department, Ellen Boesenburg, and her husband, Mohamed Aly, were temporary caretakers of Ali Makki's work, housed at a local refugee support organization, American Civic. My students had mounted on the walls of the gallery side by side with the work of Ali Makki all of the artwork produced by children working on the mural in the bi-weekly art workshops they had convened. It is difficult to describe how emotionally moving these experiences were for all participants. At our art show we attempted a kind of question-and-answer-style gallery talk. An eleven-year-old Puerto Rican boy commented about one of Ali Makki's particularly foreboding works featuring anguished-looking parents far removed from a baby in a cradle, "They are afraid that they won't be able to protect their children."

There has been marvelous education for all of us in contempo-rary issues of representation and identity. For instance, one of our participating Kurdish teenagers objected at the second pancake supper to the consensus it appeared the families were reaching (actually against the hopes of my students) about having the scen-ery from a folktale dictated by a local Somali mother and translated by her son *unify* the larger mural. This young woman, S., did not want her diary pages describing persecution at the hands of Saddam's soldiers presented in the mural as part of what she dismissively (and accurately) characterized as *a fairy tale!* After much heated discussion a new consensus was reached: S. would be pic-tured in front of a tree holding up her diary pages. She and the tree would be surrounded by barbed wire, both to separate her from the mural's more pastoral themes and to wage a protest against the idea of a unified representation of multiple life stories of oppression.

Thus far we have produced four community murals and a detailed proposal for a youth credit union in the same community of the original mural. Some of us, including my own family and myself, also participated in the rebuilding of a church in Greensboro, Alabama firebombed by the Ku Klux Klan. One student and I met with a number of local black ministers and representatives from their churches before pursuing this project, and only after hearing a consensus that such a project could help spearhead local anti-racism activism did we proceed.

A collection of folktales and more personal stories from the countries of origin of local new immigrant families has been compiled into a reader for use in one of the two elementary schools that have participated in cultural histories murals. One project that we could not get appropriate funding to pursue will hopefully inspire a future group of Social Action as Curriculum students to try again: students planned to visit individual homes at the same housing authority residence that supported the first mural in order to collect fragments of music created by and/or listened to by family members, including children. A local jazz musician would work with my students and community members to combine these fragments into a jazz composition to be performed at the local elementary school.

The Museum of Social Advocacy as Art

In my third and most recent experience teaching this course my students not only pursued activists projects, but also mounted a museum called the Museum of Social Advocacy as Art, in which they shared their projects with the local community as a kind of political performance piece. A visitors' guide written collaboratively by me and my student Lizabeth Cain oriented the teachers, families, university faculty, and other community members who attended the museum during its one-day installation. Featured below, the guide conveys the way the course's themes elaborated in this chapter expressed themselves in the students' choice of and orientation to their projects.

Visitors' guide to The Rhythm of Compassion: A Museum of Social Advocacy as Art

The Culminating project of Social Action as Curriculum, a core course in the social justice–focused Master's programs in elementary education, SUNY Binghamton's School of Education and Human Development Sunday, April 29, 2001, BU Classroom space above the Lost Dog Café, Water and Henry Streets, Binghamton, New York.

Directions for enjoying our museum, designed, installed and enacted by the students in consultation with artist Jolaine Gee, as a three-part "dwelling" with a living room, a heart, and a street:

Enter the museum by elevator so all of us have the same beginning experience, whatever our abilities and disabilities.

Take inspiration from the poetry of children whose writing was facilitated by both Bobbette Albin and Deb Pomeroy. Sit down at the writing center or take a clipboard and try your hand at an "I'm From" poem, or "I Wish" poem either now or later.

Check out the poetry book. With Deb's facilitation, a fourth-grade class from Maine Memorial Elementary School in Maine, New York, explored homelessness and created this book. Proceeds go to the National Coalition for the Homeless to support the costs associated with a homeless child's meeting with legislators to advocate for herself and her family. See Deb's video in the "living room."
Then turn left into

"The Heart"
Please join the drum circle when you can. Our teaching drummers will stop periodically to offer basic instruction. Contemplate what it means to become more aware of the rhythms of our own bodies, and the common beat of our hearts. Use the materials in the alcove to create a collage that captures your conception of compassion.

"The 'Living' Room"
We learned in our course that heavy television watchers are more afraid of other people and have less faith in our ability to heal the world than those who watch less heavily. But this television watching experience is different: we encourage you to sit down in front of the monitors and get comfortable.

On the first monitor Anthony Gayle speaks from his own experience as an African American male, offering you his perspective on the injustice of the Rockefeller laws. We hope you will be moved to follow his footsteps into the street, where other students will urge you to sign our petition to repeal them.

On the next monitor Amy Miranda expresses the frustration that many new advocates feel when first encountering an obvious injustice: others don't necessarily see it! Here Amy addresses the pattern of people struggling to get off welfare being fired from jobs arbitrarily, just before they become eligible for benefits. Follow Amy's footsteps to the street, where she has overcome her initial frustration and pursues her "next step" in advocacy.

Discrimination, wage and hour violations, and other breaches of our employment laws are common in our society. Through education of the employer captured on the next monitor, Rhonda Khublin has advocated for the rights of employees. Through education of employees, she has provided tools for self-advocacy.

In her work with "Free the Children" Sandy Gofran facilitates the making of films like the one on view today, showing U.S. children as advocates for children in developing countries forced to work for little money to produce the clothes we wear. Follow her footsteps to the street and take a first action by signing her petition to make U.S. multinationals responsible for enforcement of U.S. standard child labor laws.

Brian Woodhouse and Anthony Gayle invited boys in a detention center to write poetry with them. Read their work on the copies provided or listen to their own recitations on the tape recorder.

Erika Morton's work has focused on the benefits of learning music by ear, one of them being a greater likelihood of participation in orchestras by blind musicians. Meet the composer and listen on headphones to this beautiful piece that can easily accommodate blind children in an elementary school orchestra. Money from our grant is helping the artist get the piece published.

View Raquel Nayor's photos of local and national cases of animal abuse. Get info on humane treatment of household pets. Learn what to do when you encounter abuse, write a letter to help eliminate puppy mills, or donate to local animal shelters.

Learn about the Binghamton–El Charcón Sister City Project, which was formed in 1992 to lend moral, financial, personal, and political support to the tiny community of El Charcón in El Salvador. The cards on sale here, designed by Kelly Dufresne, originated as student drawings in a contest sponsored by the BECSCP under the theme of "La Solidaridad," or "Solidarity." All proceeds from the sale of these cards will go directly to the BECSCP in support of quality education for the children of El Charcón.

In a closely related project, Grant Shulman, Kelly Dufresne, and Kelly Craft worked with the Newark Valley Historical Society Youth Interpreters to create this beautiful quilt that features the original drawings by children from El Charcón. Our raffle will raise money and awareness for El Charcón, which recently suffered severe earthquake damage. Observe members of the youth group, in period costume, as they skillfully finish the quilt. Then join in miniature quilt and candle-making, revaluing the folk art tradition of Newark Valley as well as specifically supporting the work of the Billings-Bement Farmstead.

"The Street"
Work with us toward repeal of the Rockefeller laws, which unfairly target minorities and people of low income by imposing mandatory sentences for first-time, nonviolent drug offenses without the possibility of parole, resulting in a huge increase in prisons but no money for treatment and prevention programs.

Use the map to learn which clothing labels are particularly offensive with regard to child labor practices. Support Free the Children's work to internationalize child labor laws with your signature on Sandy's letters.

Alexis Elman and Farrah Napack have focused on advocacy for people with disabilities. Exploring with young children their conceptions about blindness, Alexis and Farrah have arranged for Maria Dibble, director of the Southern Tier Independence Center, to speak to them from her experience as a blind person and advocate for people with disabilities. The children's advocacy tree contains their vision for healing the world, translated into braille.

Let poet Brian teach you how to juggle, a necessary life skill for activists!

Before you leave the museum, Maria Dibble invites you to hear her understanding of our museum project as a community member who served as consultant.

Note from Kelly C.: Howard Gardner popularized the Theory of Multiple Intelligences in 1983 in his book, *Frames of Mind*. Please take personally the projection of different intelligences on the walls of our museum: visual-spatial, bodily-kinesthetic, intrapersonal, interpersonal, musical-rhythmic, verbal-linguistic, logical-mathematical, and naturalist.

As future educators we value all intelligences and see hope for social renewal in a more balanced appreciation of all of them in schools and in the society. Do you or people you love have an undervalued special intelligence? Consider advocacy! One possible first step:

Voice your concerns about high-stakes testing in New York State public schools at a meeting called by area concerned parents, teachers, and students:

FORUM ON HIGH-STAKES TESTING
THURSDAY EVENING, MAY 10
DECKER ROOM OF THE NEW BINGHAMTON DOWNTOWN
PUBLIC LIBRARY

Conclusion

The hope of this book is that our students as teachers will initiate the children in their classrooms into *social action as curriculum*, recognizing in Dewey's "mind-body in wholeness of operation" the spirit of healthy human life I first identified in Judith Davis's classroom. (See Chapter 1.) Thus in our internal planning of our social justice–focused master's program in elementary education at SUNY Binghamton, we have moved from offering social action as curriculum as an elective to making it a required core course. In the near future, our plan is to offer it in coordination with our students' final student teaching internship, requiring that the activists project be enacted in cooperation with sponsoring classroom teachers and their colleagues and children.

One of the things our students learn while engaging in *social action as curriculum* is the reality that there are many different and complex identities hiding behind the white middle-class female one that presents itself initially as "the identity" of the majority of our students and the majority of teachers. Our students are frequently working class; some have known poverty. Most have had relatives who suffered acute oppression as ethnics, farmers, and/or impoverished immigrants. Our students of color have not necessarily consciously processed their own experiences through appropriately supportive challenging text that links their oppression to the oppression of other groups, nor have they examined their own feelings of internalized victimization. Our male students have almost never considered the constraints of being male in this culture, nor have they typically had the support to reflect on their own typically self-limiting patterns of entitlement.

The experiences and supporting text featured in Social Action as Curriculum can help students critically explore and then turn on its head the usual interpretations progressives have made of "privilege." For it is Dewey's conception of "human life" that represents the privilege I want to offer my students and their students. My own spiritual direction for our work is to end all oppression by making such a "privileged" conception of "human life" available to everyone and therefore, no longer privileged. Those of us in teacher education need to help students construct meaning-making systems to guide our work together. These meaning-making systems re-establish the reality that all human growth projects exist within the context of limitations and obstacles that we can act on and act against, but not necessarily overcome. The investment needs to be in the intentional project of *acting*, which includes teacher responsibility for strategizing about how to make certain dialectical conceptions of human growth *thinkable* to her/his students. It's a spiritual as well as political process, and it will require "a wild patience."

Notes

Introduction

1. Maxine Greene cites C. Taylor. *Hegel and Modern Society*. Cambridge: Cambridge University Press, 1985, pp.157–60.
2. The complete quote from Barbara Christian is, "what I write and how I write is done in order to save my own life. And I mean that literally. For me literature is a way of knowing that I am not hallucinating, that whatever I feel/know is." Ellsworth cites Barbara Christian, "The Race for Theory." See bibliography.
3. The complete quote from Selvin's personal correspondence to Ellsworth is, "I too have to fight to differentiate myself from a position defined for me—whose terms are imposed on me—which limits and can destroy me—which does destroy many White men or turns them into helpless agents. . . . I as a White man/boy was not allowed—by my family, by society to be anything but cut off from the earth and the body. That condition is not/was not an essential component or implication of my maleness."
4. Ellsworth (p. 320) borrows the term *moving about* from Trinh Minh-ha and offers the following citation:

> After all, she is this Inappropriated Other who moves about with always at least two/four gestures: that of affirming "I am like you" while pointing insistently to the difference; and that of reminding "I am different" while unsettling every definition of otherness arrived at. (From Trinh T. Minh-ha, "Introduction," *Discourse, 8* (fall/winter, 1986/87): p. 9.)

Chapter 1

1. Introduction to *The Use of the Self* by F. M. Alexander. See bibliography.
2. Preoccupation with the Disconnected, from "Body and Mind," first published in the Bulletin of the NY Academy of Medicine, 1928. See bibliography.
3. Reference to the title of Wexler's book, *Holy Sparks: Social Theory, Education and Religion*.
4. When I student taught in Wayne County in 1972–73 the migrant worker population was African American and whole families came up together. A combination of factors, including African American parents encouraging their

children to get an education and reject migrant work; Florida Disney World's creation of jobs; the 1986 Immigration Reform and Control Act IRCA, which gave legal residency status to agricultural workers but not to their families; and the mid-80s cocaine addiction crisis in Florida, including racist responses to that crisis by northern growers, led to a shift in the migrant population to Mexican men without their families. By the time I returned to Judith Davis's classroom in 1990, there were few children of migrant workers in the school. This is actually changing at the present time, as more Mexican families endure the five-year-plus wait for residency status.

5. Unfortunately, *My Country School Diary* is out of print. The four-year diary (1937–1941) of a Dewey-educated, well-supervised country school teacher, Julia Weber Gordon, this text represents a gold mine of resources for elementary students and educators dedicated to promoting democracy and social justice. My hope is that enough public attention to this text might move its last publisher, HarperCollins, to reissue it.

Chapter 4

1. This is Marilyn Cochran-Smith's conception of antiracist teacher education.

References

Angelou, Maya. 1982. *I know why the caged bird sings*. New York: Ballantine Books.

Anyon, Jean. 1981. Social class and school knowledge. *Curriculum Inquiry*, 11(1): 3–42.

Apple, Michael. 1996. Education, identity and cheap French fries. In *Cultural politics and education*. New York: Teachers College Press.

Ashton-Warner, Sylvia. 1986. *Teacher*. New York: Touchstone (Simon & Schuster).

Barclay, Craig,, and Hodges, Rosemary. 1990. Compositing oneself in autobiographical memories. *Psychologie Française*.

Baylor, Byrd. 1975. *The desert is theirs*. New York: Scribner's.

Becker, Ernest. 1973. *The denial of death*. New York: The Free Press.

Benjamin, Jessica. 1988. *The bonds of love: psychoanalysis, feminism, and the problem of domination*. New York: Pantheon Books.

Birchman, David F. 1997. *A green horn blowing*. New York: Lothrop, Lee and Shepard Books (Morrow).

Bowers, Charles. A. 1987. *Elements of a post-liberal theory of education*. New York: Teachers College Press.

Brown, Margaret Wise. 1942. *The runaway bunny*. New York: Harper & Row.

———. 1947. *Goodnight moon*. New York: Harper & Row.

Burman, Erica. 1994. *Deconstructing developmental psychology*. New York and London: Routledge.

Christensen, Linda. 2000. *Reading, writing, and rising up*. Milwaukee: Rethinking Schools Ltd.

Christian, B. 1987. The race for theory. *Cultural Critique*, 6: 51-63 (spring).

Ciardi, J. 1959. *How does a poem mean?* Boston: Houghton-Mifflin.

Clay, M. 1985. *The early detection of reading difficulties*. Third edition. Portsmouth, NH: Heinemann.

Delpit, Lisa. 1995. *Other peoples' children*. New York: The New Press.

Dewey, John. 1902/1990. *The school and society the child and the curriculum: An expanded edition with a new introduction by Philip W. Jackson*. Chicago: University of Chicago Press.

———. 1928. Preoccupation with the disconnected. From "Body and Mind." First published in the *Bulletin of the NY Academy of Medicine*, 1928. "Body and Mind" is included within *The complete works of John Dewey: Later works, volume 3: 1927–1928, Essays, reviews, miscellany*, 25–40. Southern Illinois University Press. Retrieved May 28, 2000, from the John Dewey and the Alexander Technique website, http://www.alexandercenter.com/jd/index.html.

———. 1932. Introduction to *The use of the self* by F. M. Alexander. First published by E. P. Dutton, 1932. Retrieved May 28, 2000, from the John Dewey and the Alexander Technique website.

Douglas, Ann. 1977. *The feminization of American culture*. New York: Avon Books.

Dyson, Anne H. 1993. *Social worlds of children learning to write in an urban primary school*. New York and London: Teachers College Press.

Ellsworth, Elizabeth. 1989. Why doesn't this feel empowering? Working through the repressive myths of critical pedagogy. In L. Stone (ed.), *The education feminist reader*, pp. 300–327. New York and London: Routledge.

Erickson, Frederick. 1986. Qualitative methods on research in teaching. *Institute for Research on Teaching*, pp. 119–61.

Fadiman, Anne. 1997. *The spirit catches you and you fall down: A Hmong child, her American doctors, and the collision of two cultures*. New York: The Noonday Press.

Feinber, Walter. 1972. Progressive education and social planning. *Teachers College Record*, 73:485–505.

Gee, James P. 1996. *Social linguistics and literacies: Ideology in discourses*. London and Bristol: Taylor and Francis.

Glass, G. G. 1973. *Teaching decoding as separate from reading: Freeing reading from non-reading to the advantage of both*. Garden City, NY: Adelphi University Press.

Goodenow, Ronald. 1977. Racial and ethnic tolerance in John Dewey's educational and social thought: the Depression years. *Educational Theory*, 27:48–63.

Greene, Maxine. 1988. *The dialectic of freedom*. New York and London: Teachers College Press.

———. 1995. *Releasing the imagination: Essays on education, the arts, and social change*. San Francisco: Jossey-Bass Publishers.

Grumet, Madeleine. 1988. *Bitter milk: Women and teaching*. Amherst: University of Massachusetts Press.

Hamilton, Mary L., and Pinnegar, Stefinee. 2000. On the threshold of a new century: Trustworthiness, integrity, and self-study in teacher education. *Journal of Teacher Education*, 51:3, May/June.

hooks, bell. 1992. Revolutionary black women. In *Black looks: Race and representation*. Boston: South End Press.

Katz, Michael B. 1971. *Class, bureaucracy, and schools: The illusion of educational America*. New York: Praeger. Chapter 3: 107–45.

Kingsolver, Barbara. 1990. *Animal dreams*. New York: HarperCollins.

Kliebard, H. 1987. *The struggle for the American curriculum 1893–1958*. New York: Routledge.

Ladson Billings, Gloria. 1994. *The dreamkeepers: Successful teachers of African American children*. San Francisco: Jossey-Bass Publishers.

Lather, Patti. 1986. Research as Praxis. *Harvard Educational Review*, 56/3 (August):257–77.

Loewen, James. 1995. *Lies my teacher told me*. New York: Touchstone (Simon and Schuster).

Memmi, Albert. 1965. *The colonizer and the colonized*. Boston: Beacon Press.

Obama, Barack. 1995. *Dreams from my father*. New York: Kodansha America.

National Labor Committee. 1996. video: *Mickey Mouse goes to Haiti: Walt Disney and the science of exploitation.* 17 min.

National Labor Committee. 1995. video: *Zoned for slavery: The child behind the label.* 23 min.

Paley, Vivian G. 1990. *The boy who would be a helicopter: The uses of storytelling in the classroom.* Cambridge and London: Harvard University Press.

Pittenger, Mark. 1997. A world of difference: Constructing the "underclass" in progressive America. *American Quarterly*, 49:26–65.

Regenspan, Barbara. March 2000. Our Town section, second article. *The Bookpress: The Newspaper of the Literary Arts* (Ithaca, NY), 10/2:7, 11.

Riggs, Marlon. 1987. film: *Ethnic notions.*

Ringgold, Faith. 1991. *Tar beach.* New York: Crown Publishers.

Ruddick, Sara. 1989. *Maternal thinking: Toward a politics of peace.* New York: Ballantine Books.

Rushdie, Salman. 1999. *Salman Rushdie's Haroun and the Sea of Stories.* Adapted by Tim Supple and David Tushingham. London: Faber and Faber.

Shulman, Lee S. 1987. Knowledge and teaching: Foundations of the new reform. *Harvard Educational Review*, 57:1 (February).

Slapin, Beverly, and Seale, Doris. 1992. *Through Indian eyes: The native experience in books for children.* Philadelphia and Gabriola Island, BC: New Society Publishers.

Slattery, Patrick. 2001. The educational researcher as artist working within. *Qualitative Inquiry*, 7/3 (spring/summer).

Sleeter, C. E. 1999. *Making choices for multicultural education: Five approaches to race, class, and gender.* Third edition. New York: John Wiley.

Suleiman, Susan R. 1990. *Subversive intent: Gender, politics, and the avant-garde.* Cambridge and London: Harvard University Press.

Weber Gordon, Julia. 1946. *My country school diary.* New York: Harper and Bros.

Wexler, Philip. 1996. *Holy sparks: Social theory, education and religion.* New York: St. Martin's Press.

Willinsky, John. 1990. *The new literacy: Redefining reading and writing in the schools.* New York and London: Routledge.

Wulf, Steve. 1996. The glow from a fire. *Time Magazine*, 49, January 8.

Index

A

ACS. *See* Alternative Community
    School
activism
    assignment encouraging, 120–22
    author's, 6–8, 9, 30, 119, 130, 131–33
    importance for education students,
        46–47, 120–21
    involving teachers in, 30, 148
    schools and, 119, 129
    in teacher education, 6–7, 132, 135,
        137
    See also social action as curriculum;
        Social Action as Curriculum course
Alexander, Diane, 60, 61–67
Alexander, F. M., *The Use of the Self,* 40
Alexander, Henry, 60, 61–66, 67
Alexander Technique, defined, 40
Alternative Community School,
    Ithaca, New York (ACS), 119, 129
Aly, Mohamed, 163
Angelou, Maya, *I Know Why the Caged
    Bird Sings,* 156
Anyon, Jean, "Social Class and School
    Knowledge," 153
Apple, Michael, "Education, Identity
    and Cheap French Fries," 155
assignments
    to encourage activism, 120–22
    to enrich and explain theory and
        ideas, 60, 115
    as front-loaded, 147–49, 160–61
    to increase understanding of others,
        116
    paper on a film, 159–60
    to teach practical skills, 56–57
    See also study guides
Ausbey, Henry J., Reverend, 85–86
    input of, 76
    involvement in cultural history
        mural, 162
Ausbey, Henry J., Reverend, "Cotton
    Pickin' Time," poem, 84–85
    used in classroom, 86–89, 99, 108

B

Barclay, Craig, 12, 108
Baylor, Byrd, *The Desert Is Theirs,* 38
Becker, Ernest, *The Denial of Death,* 138
Benjamin, Jessica, 13
"best-practices" composite, 79–80
Binghamton University, social justice–
    focused master's program in
    elementary education
    constant revision of, 117
    curriculum, 26
    ideal program, 46–47
    as ideologically committed, 56, 128–29
    lessons used in, rationale for, 32–33
    teaching of key works, 45
    work to develop students' self-
        reflective and caring capacities, 46
    See also Social Action as Curriculum
        course
Boesenburg, Ellen, 163
Bookpress, 119–20
    author's article for, and response,
        121, 131–32
Bowers, Chuck, 1–2
Burman, Erica, 54

C

children in the classroom
immigrant, and their stories, 70
language experience stories, 27, 28–29
nurturing of, teaching prospective teachers about, 112–13
as part of real community, 109
shaping attitudes and behavior of, 94–98
stories about making connections, 110–11
teacher treatment of, 4, 94–96, 97–98
children's families and communities
involvement of, 80, 84, 91
parents, communication with, 3
stories of, 8, 31
Christensen, Linda, 31; *Reading, Writing, and Rising Up*, 154
Christian, Barbara, 17, 18, 103, 171n2
Citizens' Planning Alliance, Ithaca, New York, 119, 130, 132
class activities
collective story writing, 5
construction project, 92, 105–6
"human life" experiences, 28
play, 93, 104–6
poetry workshop, 88–91
variety of, 3, 80, 91, 97
writing exercises, 4, 99, 103
writing support groups, 102–4
See also children in the classroom; curriculum, arts-focused; group meetings; photography in the schools; "urban-rural" unit
classrooms, multi-age
curriculum for, 79–80
organizing principles, 80–82
teaching team, perspective and practices, 82–83, 87
Cochran-Smith, Marilyn, 172n1
connectedness, theme of, 77, 90, 101, 108–9
curriculum

children's participation in, 82, 87, 107
as part of community life and activism, 118–19, 135–36
See also social action as curriculum
curriculum, arts-focused
computer use, 106–7
concept of connectedness and community, 87–88, 113
photography workshop, 100
"practice for . . ." and "the real thing," 83, 90–91, 100, 104, 110
principles for, 79, 80, 82–83
teaching artistic techniques, 98–100
value of, 113–14
curriculum courses
assignments for, 56–57
dealing with richness of materials, 38
projects for, 37–38
curriculum-making
attempt to spiral teaching into the community, 148
Christensen and, 154
Davis's model, 24, 25, 30, 38, 41
exercises for, 56–57, 115
future, importance of conversation, 38
influence of Dewey, 24, 145
influence of Ruddick, 24–25
"integrated day" program, 30

D

Davis, Judith
author's early training with, 1–2, 3, 7, 27–30
author's research with, 11, 14
in class, 29–30
curriculum-making, importance of, 24, 25, 30, 38
elementary curriculum, bases, 25, 26, 41, 44
philosophy, 1, 4, 43
teaching themes, 30–31, 38, 168
Delpit, Lisa, 4, 153

deconstruction, concept of, 66–67
Dewey, John, 137
  concept of mind-body in action, 23,
    25, 26, 31, 138, 145, 168
  connections with feminist thinking,
    13, 25
  division of labor, 6, 31, 32–33, 77,
    125, 128
  evaluation of, 26, 31, 39–44
  "human life" concept, 5–6, 31, 32, 38,
    39–41, 169
  and practice of Alexander, 40
  use of human imagination for
    growth, 5–6, 124–25, 127
  See also mind-body connections,
    Dewey and
Dewey, John, School and Society The
  Child and the Curriculum, The
  drawbacks, 47, 49
  as inspiration for students, 25–26
  as life-text, 49–50, 149–50
  study guide for, 52–55
  teaching of, 45, 47–49
  use in curriculum-planning, 115–16
dialectic of freedom
  as concept of Greene, 41, 43, 59, 70–
    71, 76
  described and applied, 119, 133–34,
    138, 152
  importance of activism, 133, 152
dominant culture, concept of
  and education students, 46, 137
  influence on curriculum, 11, 68
  problems for those outside, 29
  understanding, 43
Dyson, Anne Haas, 102–3

E

education, critical theorists' writings on
  as not always useful and practical,
    15, 137
  as often inaccessible, 16–17, 137
  problems of judgmentalism, 17
  as promoting privilege, 137

education, social issues to be
  considered
  environmentalism, 120
  Native American concerns, 39
  See also racism and classism
elementary education today
  appropriate foundations for quality
    in, 18, 19
  classroom, messages of dominant
    culture, 43–44
  needed and suggested changes and
    reforms, 75–76, 142–44
  present program, rethinking of, 46
  progressive methods, discouraging
    results, 136–37
  racism and classism in, 16
  social foundations knowledge, as
    marginalized, 46
  what is often suppressed, 32
  See also "social reconstructionism";
    social reconstruction programs;
    students of elementary education
Edwards, Willie, Jr., crime against, 61–
  65, 66
Ellsworth, Elizabeth, "Why Doesn't
  This Feel Empowering?" 17–20, 102–3
Ethnic Notions, film, 106, 155
  assignment on, 159–60
  reactions to and benefits from 160–61

F

Fadiman, Anne, The Spirit Catches You
  and You Fall Down, assignment on, 116
feminist perspectives
  in Dewey, 13, 25
  maternal influence, concept of, 12–
    13, 24, 87, 107–8, 111–13
  post-structuralist, influence of, 10,
    16, 18–19
  psychoanalytic, influence of, 13
  use in understanding literature, 146
Foundations of Multiculturalism
  course, 38
Fuerstein, Carl, 67–68

G

Geertz, Clifford, 120, 131
"Glass Analysis," 28, 103
Gogol, Nicolay, "The Nose," 2, 4
Gowin, D. Bob, 72
Green Horn Blowing, A, 89, 99
Greene, Maxine, 15, 31, 39
Greene, Maxine, *Dialectic of Freedom, The*
    evaluation of, 57, 59, 138
    as inspiration for author, 76, 120–21
    notion of dialectic of freedom, 41, 43,
        59, 70–71, 76
    student difficulties with, and
        response to, 57, 59, 71, 73–74
    study guide for, and discussion, 72–
        75
    teaching of, 45, 59, 67, 68–69, 71, 74
    use of accompanying texts, 59, 74, 138
    See also Ku Klux Klan widow article;
        "situatedness," concept of
group meetings
    examples of, 91–92
    process of engaging children, 93–94
    shaping children's attitudes and
        behavior, 94–98
    understanding children's behavior,
        96–97
Grumet, Madeleine, 13

H

Hadziabdic, Sead
    achievement in photography, 99, 101
    participation on school, 91, 100–101,
        108
Hartsock, Eleanor, 146
Hine, Lewis, 86, 100, 101
Hodges, Rosemary, 12, 108
hooks, bell, *Black Looks,* 40–41

I

IWP. *See* International Workers Party

immigrants
    children of, and their stories, 8, 70
    learning about, 8, 9, 100–102
International Workers Party (IWP),
    author and, 7–10
Internet, role of, 106–7
Ithaca, New York, City of, Southwest
    development plan, 122–23, 125–30
    opposition campaign, and author's
        involvement, 119, 127–29

K

Kingsolver, Barbara, *Animal Dreams,*
    115, 136
    assignments for, 145–47, 150–52
    content and themes, 139, 145, 153–54
    other materials used with, 152–55,
        159–60
    as teaching tool, 144–45, 148–49
    use of, rationale, 138, 140–44
Kingsolver, Barbara, *Poisonwood Bible,*
    The, 140
Ku Klux Klan, bombing, 164
Ku Klux Klan widow article, 61–66
    discussion about, 66–67
    use of, 60

L

Lewis Hine photography exhibit, 86,
    87, 88
    described, 100
    used in class programs, 99, 101–2
life-text: described, 49
    examples of, 49–50, 149–50
    learning from, 149
    use and importance of, 58, 59, 74,
        118, 138
literature
    appreciation, in learning situation,
        146–47
    importance in classroom, 2, 3, 4
    multicultural, use in curriculum, 115

poetry and connectedness, 87–88
stories of school children and their families, 8, 31, 70
use in courses, and examples, 34, 36, 38–39, 49–50, 59, 74–75, 118, 120, 138, 139, 155
Loewen, James, 31; *Lies My Teacher Told Me*, 34, 36

M

Makki, Ali, 163
Memmi, Albert, 141–42
Mickey Mouse Goes to Haiti, film, 152
migrant workers
changes in population, 172n4
children, teaching of, 27–28
connections with, 30
as source of information and learning, 88–89
mind-body connections, Dewey and
for curriculum, 26, 40–41, 145
and feminist theory, 13, 25
idea of thinking and doing, 31, 75, 168
importance for parallel practices approach, 23–24, 44, 138
Minh-hah, Trinh, 171n4
Moss, Joy, 28
mural painting projects, 117
as involving various communities, 162
in New York City, 7
See also Saratoga Cultural Histories Mural
Museum of Social Advocacy as Art, 153, 164
Museum of Social Advocacy as Art, visitors' guide to
text, 165–68
writing of, 135, 136, 164

N

Nicholson, Steve, 132–33

Nossiter, Alan, article on Ku Klux Klan widow, 60–72

O

Obama, Barack, *Dreams from My Father*
content and themes, 139, 159–60
study guide for, 156–59
use of, rationale, 138, 155–56

P

Paley, Vivian, *The Boy Who Would Be a Helicopter*, 54
parallel practices
explanation of, and purpose, 135
and role of mind-body connections, 23–24, 44, 138
value of, 38, 137
photography in the schools
experience with photographer, 100–101
provision of cameras and picture-taking experience, 100
related projects for children, 102
See also Lewis Hine photography exhibit
pinchpot lesson
background, 32–33
class activity and ensuing discussions, 33–38
use of, to illustrate about community, 109–11
use of, in teaching classes, 38–39
value of, 41–42
play, role of
the block area, 104
play as practice for real life, 104–6

R

racism and classism
consideration of, in class, 67–69, 70

and in critical theory, 17
in education, 16
in literary and film examples, 106, 139, 153, 155–56, 159–60
as needed topics to address in courses, 17–18
as personal issues for education students, 66–68, 168–69
readers, reading: decoding for, 28
"Glass Analysis," 28, 103
See also words
Regenspan, Barbara, career and thinking
aims, 25, 26, 31, 149, 169
commitment to social justice, 76–77
connections with families, 9, 10–11, 31
early social and political activity, 6–8, 9
educational training and experience, 1–6, 10–11, 24, 28, 45
individual contributions to and influences on, 1–2, 4, 5, 24–25, 26
later activism and experience in community, 30, 119, 130, 131–33
student-teaching experience, 1–2, 27, 172n4
thesis research, 11, 12–13
visceral concerns, 8–9, 10, 12, 18
and "wholeness of labor," 25, 31, 32
Regenspan, Barbara, teaching examples and methods
awareness of social problems, 141–42
classroom activity and ensuing discussion, 33–34
encouragement of activism, 37, 120–21, 137
encouragement of self-reflection, 46, 70, 71
involvement in local cause and writing about it, 120, 130, 131–32
reading aloud, 55
reference to relevant books, 34, 59, 74, 116, 120, 138

showing work, 35
small group discussions, 34–35, 56, 146
See also assignments; parallel practices; pinchpot lesson; social action as curriculum; Social Action as Curriculum course; study guides
Regenspan, Barbara, *Parallel Practices*
background, 1–2
desired results, 168
inspirations for, 8
structure, 20–21
Riggs, Marlon, *Ethnic Notions*, 106, 155, 159–61
Ringgold, Faith, *Tar Beach*, 115
Ruddick, Sara, 19
concept of maternal influence, 12–13, 24
maternal storytelling, 87, 107, 112, 146
roots of misogyny, 14–15
theme of connectedness, 77, 90, 101
Rushdie, Salman, 121–22
approach and humor of, 122
Rushdie, Salman, *Haroun and the Sea of Stories* and dramatic adaptation, 2, 19, 119, 132
assignment based on, 119–20, 131
message of hope, 129–30
themes, and political import, 123–29

S

Saratoga Cultural Histories Mural, 76, 85–86
consequences and benefits, 163–64
participants in, 161–63
Selvin, Albert, 18, 171n3
"situatedness," concept of, 15, 60
explained, 58–59, 142, 152
Shange, Ntozake, *For Colored Girls Who Have Considered Suicide When the Rainbow Is Enuf*, 158
social action as curriculum

parallel practices for, 135
as community principle, 20–21, 134
as principle in education, 117, 168
Social Action as Curriculum course,
37
integration of activist focus, 47, 131,
138
literature for, 138, 139
projects connected to, 153, 161, 164
purposes and aims for, 148, 160–61
as required core course, 168
what is learned, 168–69
See also mural painting projects;
Museum of Social Advocacy as Art
"social reconstructionism"
defined and characterized, 82
practices that support, 82–83
See also social reconstruction
programs
social reconstruction programs
curriculum-making, 25, 26, 137
importance of Dewey for, 40–42
involving children as well as
teachers, 82, 87
need to teach about political and
social activity, 6–7, 132, 135, 137
need for social awareness, 141
teaching of, 46
value of community, 108–9
See also parallel practices
students of elementary education
importance of activism, 46–47,
120–21
importance of parallel practices for,
26
lesson in collectivity, 121
mistrust of theory, 16
need to avoid cynicism, 142–43
need for self-reflection and understanding, 46, 55, 71
racism and classism as personal
issues, 66–68, 168–69
themes for, and ways to educate, 31
tools for, 50–52
study guides

content and reasons for using, 50–52
example of, using Dewey, 52–55
example of, using Greene, 72–75
example of, using Obama, 156–59
reviewing of, and group input, 55–57
Suleiman, Susan, 13

T

Taylor, Charles, 15, 58
teacher education, social justice–
focused
bases for, 23–24
need to protect, 131
See also Binghamton University
teacher-educators
lesson in involvement in local issues
and writing about it, 120–21
need to avoid cynicism, 142–43
need for compassion and commitment, 135
need to nurture capacity of joy and
wonder in aspiring teachers, 15
need for self-reflection and understanding, 55, 71
and theme of teacher's personal
growth, 113–14
work needed for, 19–20
teachers
as advocates and activists, 30, 148
limitations and challenges for, 143–44
needed training for, 5
powerfully alive, influence of, 14
problems of recognition, 143–44
See also children in classroom
teaching methods and tools
teaching team, 82–83, 87
wordbooks, 3, 86–87, 99, 104
See also assignments; curriculum,
arts-focused; group meetings;
pinchpot lesson; study guides
Through Indian Eyes, 34, 38–39

U

"urban-rural" unit
  examples of participation in, 88–89
  museum installation project, 106
  research sources and projects for, 91,
    100, 106
  as tied to other classroom activities,
    86–87, 92

V

Vines, Mr., 4–5

W

Weber, Lillian, 27, 30
Weber Gordon, Julia, *My Country
  School Diary*, 38, 54
  as "companion text," 36, 50, 74–75
Wexler, Philip, 27
Wood, Jim, 4
words
  and different languages, 5
  and "Glass Analysis," 28
  importance for history, 31
  rhyming words, 3
  wordbooks, 3, 86–87, 99, 104
writing support groups
  concept of maternal storytelling,
    107–8, 112–13
  faculty research on, 102–104
  functions, 103
  importance of writing in schools,
    107–8
  support for autobiographical history,
    108–9
  use of other lessons in 110–11

Z

Zoned for Slavery, film, 152

Studies in the Postmodern Theory of Education

General Editors
Joe L. Kincheloe & Shirley R. Steinberg

Counterpoints publishes the most compelling and imaginative books being written in education today. Grounded on the theoretical advances in criticalism, feminism, and postmodernism in the last two decades of the twentieth century, Counterpoints engages the meaning of these innovations in various forms of educational expression. Committed to the proposition that theoretical literature should be accessible to a variety of audiences, the series insists that its authors avoid esoteric and jargonistic languages that transform educational scholarship into an elite discourse for the initiated. Scholarly work matters only to the degree it affects consciousness and practice at multiple sites. Counterpoints' editorial policy is based on these principles and the ability of scholars to break new ground, to open new conversations, to go where educators have never gone before.

For additional information about this series or for the submission of manuscripts, please contact:

Joe L. Kincheloe & Shirley R. Steinberg
c/o Peter Lang Publishing, Inc.
275 Seventh Avenue, 28th floor
New York, New York 10001

To order other books in this series, please contact our Customer Service Department:

(800) 770-LANG (within the U.S.)
(212) 647-7706 (outside the U.S.)
(212) 647-7707 FAX

Or browse online by series:
www.peterlangusa.com